THE 25 GREATEST

BASEBALL PLAYERS OF ALL TIME

★ **LEN BERMAN** ★

sourcebooks
jabberwocky

Published by Sourcebooks Jabberwocky, an imprint of Sourcebooks, Inc.
P.O. Box 4410, Naperville, Illinois 60567-4410
(630) 961-3900
Fax: (630) 961-2168
www.jabberwockykids.com

Library of Congress Cataloging-in-Publication Data
Berman, Len.
  25 greatest baseball players of all time / by Len Berman.
      p. cm.
1. Baseball players—Rating of—United States. 2. Baseball players—United States—Statistics. 3. Baseball players—United States—Biography. I. Title. II.
Title: Twenty-five greatest baseball players of all time.
  GV865.A1.B48 2010
  796.3570922—dc22
  [B]

2010014378

Source of Production: Oceanic Graphic Printing, Kowloon, Hong Kong
Date of Production: March 2012
Run Number: 17279

Printed and bound in China.
OGP 10 9 8 7 6 5 4 3

CONTENTS

INTRODUCTION

So I thought this was going to be easy. Who can't pick the 25 greatest baseball players of all time? I immediately wrote down my list. It totaled 31. Uh-oh. And that list of 31 left out some of my favorite all-time players, like Tom Seaver and Jim Palmer.

Then it struck me. I couldn't do this by myself. So I recruited a special "Blue Ribbon Panel" to help me decide—and they couldn't agree on 25 either. So I tallied up all the votes, and the top 25 made it.

There are still some major omissions. Yankee catcher Yogi Berra may have won 10 World Series and three Most Valuable Player (MVP) Awards, but he didn't make the cut. And neither did fellow Hall of Famer Nolan Ryan, despite his record seven no-hitters. Sandy Koufax was one of the all-time great pitchers, and Mariano Rivera may be the best reliever ever, but neither of them made it either. That's how tough this was.

So out of thousands of major leaguers, we have somehow whittled the list down to 25. They are the greatest of the great. See if you agree.

My Blue Ribbon Panel

My Blue Ribbon Panel consists of former players, a long-time baseball executive, and various members of the media.

- Four-time World Series champion, Yankee center fielder Bernie Williams
- Three-time All-Star pitcher for the Brooklyn Dodgers in the 1940s and 1950s, Ralph Branca
- Long-time major league executive Roland Hemond
- Emmy and Peabody Award–winning journalist Frank Deford
- Red Sox fanatic, television/film critic, and author Jeffrey Lyons
- Radio talk-show host extraordinaire Chris "Mad Dog" Russo
- Emmy Award–winning producer of *This Week in Baseball* Steve Fortunato

And special thanks to Baseball Hall of Fame president Jeff Idelson for his guidance on this project.

Forty different players received votes, and only 11 players were unanimous choices. Panelist Bernie Williams was partial to the players of his era. He voted for pitcher Pedro Martinez, saying, "The best I ever faced. In his prime... three un-hittable pitches." Ralph Branca said, "Pretty tough to leave out some of the great players. Can't we make it 30? It still would be tough to choose."

And that's the fun of it. How do you compare players from different eras? You really can't. But somehow we got it down to 25. And at the end of the book, you'll get your chance to vote for your favorites. So here we go. Play ball!

BEFORE YOU GET STARTED, HERE ARE SOME BASEBALL ABBREVIATIONS EVERY FAN SHOULD KNOW!

1B = First Base
2B = Second Base/Doubles
3B = Third Base/Triples
AB = At Bats
AL = American League
AVG = Batting Average
BA = Batting Average
C = Catcher

E = Errors
ERA = Earned Run Average
G = Games Played
H = Hits
HR = Home Runs
K = Strikeouts
L = Losses
MLB = Major League Baseball

MVP = Most Valuable Player
NL = National League
OF = Outfield
P = Pitcher
R = Runs
RBI = Runs Batted In
SS = Shortstop
W = Wins

You've probably heard of Cy Young. Every season the Cy Young Award is given to the best pitcher in the American League and the best in the National League. There's an excellent reason for that. Cy Young might have been the best pitcher ever. He certainly had the most wins. And I'm going to take a wild guess that nobody will ever match his total. It's a big deal when a pitcher wins 300 games in a career—a very big deal. It virtually guarantees that he'll make it to the Hall of Fame. Well, Cy Young won an astounding 511 games! The guy in second place, Walter Johnson, won 417—nearly 100 less. But let's start at the beginning.

Cy Young was born in Gilmore, Ohio, way back in 1867. His real name was Denton True Young. He was big by the standards of the day at 6 feet, 2 inches tall and 210 pounds. A catcher who caught his pitches thought he threw like a cyclone, so that's what they called him for awhile. "Cyclone" was shortened to "Cy," and the name stuck.

Since Cy was born in a rural town, he didn't receive much formal education. He spent his time helping out on the family farm, but he also loved to play baseball. He played for various amateur teams, and in August 1890 he joined the Cleveland Spiders, a team that played in the National League. In his very first game, he pitched a three-hitter. Not a bad debut—and a definite sign of things to come.

Cy threw the ball very hard. Of course, there were no radar guns back then, so we don't know the actual speed. But it is said that his catcher would put beefsteak inside his glove to provide extra cushion.

Cy pitched in 16 games his rookie season, and his record was a modest 9–7. In those days teams didn't have fancy bullpens, so pitchers finished what they started.

CY YOUNG

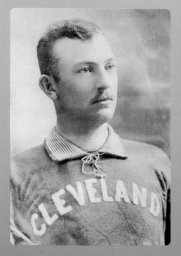

BORN: March 29, 1867

BIRTHPLACE: Gilmore, OH

HEIGHT: 6'2" **WEIGHT:** 210 lbs.

TEAMS: Cleveland Spiders, St. Louis Perfectos, Boston Americans

BATS: Right

THROWS: Right

POSITION: Pitcher

ROOKIE YEAR: 1890

CAREER ERA: 2.63

THE 25 GREATEST BASEBALL PLAYERS OF ALL TIME

CAREER HIGHLIGHTS: Won the American League Triple Crown for pitching in 1901; led the American League in ERA in 1892 and 1901; pitched a perfect game against Philadelphia in 1904; pitched a no-hitter against New York in 1908; holds the all-time career record for most wins (511); inducted into the Hall of Fame in 1937

Cy Young's record for **"OLDEST PITCHER TO THROW A NO-HITTER"** stood for 82 years, until **NOLAN RYAN** pitched a no-hitter for Texas at the age of 43. (Ryan also threw one when he was 44!)

For Cy every game that season was a complete game. His second year, his numbers popped. He had 27 wins and 22 losses, and he completed all but three of the games he started. He was just getting warmed up.

His third season was stunning. Would you believe he won 36 games? He started 49 times and pitched 48 complete games. His record was 36–12 with nine shutouts. His earned run average (ERA) was a paltry 1.93. Simply amazing.

When Cy started pitching, the pitcher's mound was 50 feet from home plate. But because of the great pitchers of the day like him, the mound was moved back to its current distance of 60 feet, 6 inches. Many pitchers had trouble making the adjustment. The year after the change was made, in 1893, even Cy Young's win production dipped. He dropped from 36 wins all the way down to 34! But in truth his ERA did go up, and his number of strikeouts went down.

And so it went for Cy, year after year. In 1901 the American League joined the major leagues. This new league needed players, so Cy jumped to the Boston Americans (which would later become the Red Sox) for the hefty sum of $3,500. He was an immediate success. He had a 33–10 record, with a miniscule ERA of 1.62 that year.

Each year it was something new. In 1902 Cy helped Harvard out as a pitching coach. Here was a kid who had never gotten past sixth grade, coaching some of the smartest young

300 WINS CLUB
Total Wins
511

men in the country. In 1903 he was part of something really new—the first-ever World Series between the Boston Americans and the Pittsburgh Pirates. Cy threw the very first pitch in the history of the World Series, but he was the losing pitcher in Game 1. He bounced back to win two games as the Americans won the Series 5 games to 3. (It was a best-of-nine World Series back then.) By the way, during the 1903 season—his best year at the plate—Cy batted .321.

The next year, 1904, Cy pitched the first perfect game in American League history. That perfect game against the Philadelphia A's was part of one of the most incredible pitching feats of all time. Cy went 45 innings without allowing a run. On top of that, he went over 24 innings without allowing a hit! That's a record that still stands today.

In 1907 Cy was 40 years old, and yet he won 21 games. The next year at the age of 41, he did it again. That year he also pitched another no-hitter, which

Cy Young (L) shakes hands with Lou Criger of the St. Louis Browns in 1909.

Cy Young winds up for one of his powerful pitches.

The **CY YOUNG AWARD** was created in 1956. It was originally given to only one pitcher in the entire major leagues. In 1967 it was decided that one pitcher from each league (American and National) could win the award.

was the third of his career. He finally retired from baseball in 1911.

All in all Cy pitched for 22 seasons. In addition to holding the record for the most wins, he still holds the records for most innings pitched and most complete games. There's a downside to all of that pitching—he also holds the record for the most losses (316)!

Cy came to Yankee Stadium to pitch in 1953. It was Game 1 of the World Series. He threw a perfect strike to Yogi Berra of the Yankees. Not bad for a guy who was 86 years old! That strike was a ceremonial pitch, 50 years after he threw the very first pitch in World Series history.

The Hall of Fame wasn't created until 1936, and you'd think Cy would be a shoo-in. But he didn't make the initial class, led by Babe Ruth and Ty Cobb. Two other pitchers were chosen: Walter Johnson and Christy Mathewson. Cy made it into Cooperstown in the second year of voting, 1937.

There's a funny trivia question I've heard: which famous baseball player is mentioned the most times on all of the Hall of Fame plaques in Cooperstown? The answer, of course, is Cy Young, because other Hall of Famers have won the Cy Young Award.

Cy's Hall of Fame plaque reads in part, "Only pitcher in first hundred years of baseball to win 500 games." But I'm almost positive he will continue to be the only pitcher to *ever* win 500 games.

DENTON T. (CY) YOUNG
CLEVELAND (N) 1890-98
ST. LOUIS (N) 1899-1900
BOSTON (A) 1901-08
CLEVELAND (A) 1909-11
BOSTON (N) 1911
ONLY PITCHER IN FIRST HUNDRED YEARS OF BASEBALL TO WIN 500 GAMES. AMONG HIS 511 VICTORIES WERE 3 NO-HIT SHUTOUTS, PITCHED PERFECT GAME MAY 5, 1904, NO OPPOSING BATSMAN REACHING FIRST BASE.

Cy Young was elected to the National Baseball Hall of Fame in Cooperstown, New York, in 1937.

Cy Young didn't wear a glove when he pitched. Many pitchers at that time didn't. He didn't start wearing one until the late 1890s.

TY COBB

O f all the great baseball players in this book, is it possible to pick the one greatest baseball player of all time? I'll reveal my vote for who I believe is the greatest baseball player of all time a little later, but my reasons for that pick go beyond baseball. If you had to choose the one greatest player purely for what he did on the field, that player most likely would be Ty Cobb.

Ty's nickname was "the Georgia Peach," but he was anything but a peach of a guy. He was downright mean and ornery, and he approached the game of baseball with a nasty attitude. His opponents hated him, and his teammates didn't like him a whole lot better. Before a game Ty would sharpen his spikes in the dugout, and then during the game he would slide into bases with his spikes high, trying to hurt players on the other team. The great manager Connie Mack called Cobb "the dirtiest player in baseball history." But nobody could dispute Ty's skill as a player. He set dozens of records in his 24-year career. And even though he stopped playing in 1928, one record still stands: his lifetime batting average of .367 is the highest ever.

But why was he so mean? Here's one explanation. His dad was a schoolteacher and a principal, and he wanted Ty to follow in his footsteps. Instead, the youngster had his heart set on baseball. When he left home to play baseball his father gave him some simple yet stern advice: "Don't come home a failure." Ty credited his father for his relentless style of play. His dad never saw him play baseball, but Ty didn't want to ever disappoint him.

Ty was born in Georgia in 1886, which means he played in the early years of our national pastime. He took the sport by storm. His drive to succeed on the field led to hours upon hours of practice. He would practice sliding until his legs couldn't take it anymore. He would wear extra-heavy boots in the winter to build up the strength in his legs. And all that practice paid off.

He made it to the major leagues as a center fielder for the Detroit Tigers just three weeks after his father's death. It was August 1905. In his very first at-bat, he hit a double off the great New York pitcher Jack Chesbro. What a start! His rookie year he batted only .240. But would you believe in the 23 seasons after that, he never batted under .300? And in three different years he batted over .400! This feat is so rare that no one has accomplished it even once since 1941, when Ted Williams batted .406.

Now I'll be the first to tell you I'm not a big fan of statistics. They are just numbers. For example, when I was a kid, Mickey Mantle was my hero. How many homers did he hit? It really didn't matter to me. In fact, I'd have to look it up. But sometimes it's hard

"Every great batter works on the theory that the pitcher is more afraid of him than he is of the pitcher."

—TY COBB

Ty Cobb gets ready for a pitch.

to ignore the numbers on a page. And that's the case with Ty Cobb. Playing for the Detroit Tigers, he led the American League in batting 12 different years, and nine of them were in a row! His first great season came in

1907. Not only did he bat .350 to lead the league, he had the most hits, runs batted in (RBIs), and stolen bases. He led the Tigers to the first of three consecutive World Series appearances. And the numbers kept on growing. In 1911 he again led the league in everything except home runs. And in 1915 he had his best season ever. He batted .420 while stealing a record 96 bases. Here's one more really important stat: when Ty retired in 1928, he held the record for most hits in a career, with 4,191. That record stood for 57 years, until Pete Rose finally broke it in 1985.

But enough about statistics. Here are some great stories that sum up the kind of player Ty Cobb really was.

Ty always annoyed his opponents. A catcher on the opposing team once told reporters that Ty wasn't as great as everyone said he was. Ty got his revenge by drawing a walk, then stealing second base, third base, and home plate on three straight pitches. During his career he stole all three bases in the same inning four different times.

Here's another story about his base running in a game against the Yankees in 1911. In the

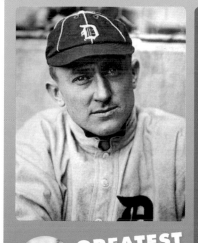

TY "THE GEORGIA PEACH" COBB

BORN: December 18, 1886

BIRTHPLACE: Narrows, GA

HEIGHT: 6'1" **WEIGHT:** 175 lbs.

TEAM: Detroit Tigers

BATS: Left

THROWS: Right

POSITION: Outfielder

ROOKIE YEAR: 1905

CAREER BATTING AVERAGE: .367

THE 25 GREATEST BASEBALL PLAYERS OF ALL TIME

CAREER HIGHLIGHTS: Won the American League Triple Crown for pitching in 1909; voted the American League MVP in 1911; holds the highest all-time career batting average (.367); inducted into the Hall of Fame in 1936

3,000 HITS CLUB

Total Hits

4,191

In 1915 Ty Cobb set the **RECORD FOR STEALING BASES**, with 96. That record stood for 47 years, until **MAURY WILLS** stole 104 bases for the L.A. Dodgers in 1962. The current record is held by **RICKEY HENDERSON**, who stole an amazing 130 bases for the Oakland Athletics in 1982.

Ty Cobb in front of the Detroit Tigers team dugout.

AMERICAN LEAGUE
TRIPLE CROWN WINNER

1909
9 HR, 115 RBIs, .377 BA

seventh inning Ty tied the game with a two-run double. The Yankee catcher, Ed Sweeney, started arguing with the umpire, and it was such a heated argument that his Yankee teammates gathered around to watch. Ty, standing on second base, realized that nobody had called time out, so he just casually walked over to third base. Then he started strolling home, pretending that he wanted to get a better view of the argument. At the last second, he slid home with the winning run, and it counted!

Here's a story about Ty's hitting. In the later stages of his career, it bothered him that Babe Ruth had become more famous. The Babe's home-run hitting had captured the fancy of the fans, and Ty didn't like it at all. Ty never tried to hit home runs, but in May 1925, he told reporters that he could hit home runs like Babe Ruth if he tried. Over the next two games, he had nine hits, and five of them were homers. It was one of the most amazing displays of hitting in baseball history.

By the time his career ended, Ty had done it all—hitting, stealing bases, breaking

Ty Cobb gets a hit during an exhibition game in Havana, Cuba.

records, and getting in numerous fights on and off the field. He was a player/manager for Detroit for six years, but he failed to win the pennant. One of the only things Ty didn't achieve by the time he retired in 1926 was winning the World Series.

But here's one more number that Ty could be proud of. When the first vote was held for induction into the Baseball Hall of Fame in 1936, the player with the highest number of votes was not Babe Ruth. It was none other than Ty Cobb.

Later in life, Ty supposedly was asked how well he would do against the current players. Ty reportedly answered that he'd bat around .310 or .315. The interviewer was shocked. Ty had been a lifetime .367 hitter and had batted over .400 three times. Why would he have such a low batting average? Ty is said to have replied, "Well, you have to remember, I'm 72 years old now."

Knowing Ty's competitive nature, he might have been serious.

What number did Ty Cobb wear?

Players didn't start wearing numbers on their uniforms until after Ty retired.

WALTER JOHNSON

Which pitcher threw the fastest of all time? We may never know for sure, but it just might have been a kid who was born in Kansas in 1887 by the name of Walter Johnson. He stood 6 feet, 1 inch and weighed 200 pounds. That's not very big by today's standards, but his fastball earned him the nickname "Big Train," and he set records that still stand today.

I'm getting way ahead of myself. Let's start much earlier. In 1905 Walter pitched in one of the most incredible high school games ever played. He pitched for Fullerton Union High School in California, and a game against Santa Ana wound up in a 0–0, fifteen-inning tie. Walter pitched all fifteen innings and struck out 27 batters! Baseball scouts took notice of this kid who threw with a sidearm delivery and possessed an amazing fastball.

When Walter graduated from high school, he moved to Idaho and started pitching for a semipro league. Word quickly spread. Since he was a small-town kid at heart, he had no interest in moving to a big city to play baseball. But the scouts kept after him, and in the summer of 1907, Walter finally broke down and signed with the Washington Senators. And what a deal it was! He received a signing bonus of $100. He also got free train fare to Washington, and a salary of $350 a month. Can you imagine how much money he would have signed for today? Now top draft picks in baseball make millions.

Walter made his debut for the Senators against the Detroit Tigers in August that same year. He was 19 years old, and the veteran players on the Tigers let the "farm boy" have it. When he walked to the mound, they made mooing sounds. But Walter was so easygoing that it didn't bother him.

Would you believe that in his very first big-league game, Walter had to pitch to Ty Cobb? It was the old nasty Cobb against the nice kid from the farm. Cobb said, "On August 2, 1907,

I encountered the most threatening sight I ever saw in the ball field. He was only a rookie. The first time I faced him I watched him take that easy windup—and then something went past me that made me flinch. The thing just hissed with danger. We couldn't touch him…every one of us knew we'd met the most powerful arm ever turned loose in a ball park." Cobb was impressed, to say the least. As for the game, Walter pitched well, but the Tigers won the game 3–2.

So how did this pitcher with the "most powerful arm" do in his first three seasons? Not bad. His earned run average (ERA) was very good, but his record after three years was just 32 wins and 48 losses. Then again, he was playing for the Washington Senators, one

One moment stands out from Walter Johnson's early seasons with the Senators: in 1908 he pitched against New York in three straight games—and he shut them out in all three! His team might have stunk, but Walter certainly did not.

The famously powerful pitching arm of Walter Johnson.

3,000 STRIKEOUTS CLUB
Total Strikeouts
3,508

of the worst teams in baseball history. In his first five years in the major leagues, the Senators finished in either last place or next-to-last every year.

Things started to change for Walter in 1910. The Senators won only 66 games that season, yet Walter won 25 of them! On top of that, his ERA was a tiny 1.36, and he led the major leagues in strikeouts with 303. He won another 25 games in 1911, and again the Senators were awful. But things really turned around in 1912 for Walter and the Senators. Walter was simply fabulous. He won 33 games! He led the league in ERA and strikeouts, and best of all, the Senators climbed all the way to second place—the best showing in franchise history.

Walter's record in 1913 was even better. He led the American League in virtually every pitching category, and won a phenomenal 36 games! Again the Senators finished in second place, and Walter was voted the Most Valuable Player (MVP) in the American League. That's a rarity for a pitcher, and yet Walter was voted MVP twice in his career.

Over the next six seasons, Walter won at least 20 games every year, and most of those seasons, he led the league in shutouts. During his career he pitched 110 shutouts.

300 WINS CLUB
Total Wins
417

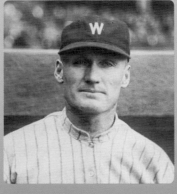

WALTER "THE BIG TRAIN" JOHNSON

THE 25 GREATEST BASEBALL PLAYERS OF ALL TIME

BORN: November 6, 1887
BIRTHPLACE: Humboldt, KS
HEIGHT: 6'1"   **WEIGHT:** 200 lbs.
TEAM: Washington Senators
BATS: Right
THROWS: Right
POSITION: Pitcher
ROOKIE YEAR: 1907
CAREER ERA: 2.17

CAREER HIGHLIGHTS: Voted the American League MVP in 1913 and 1924; won the American League Triple Crown for pitching in 1913, 1918, and 1924; led the American League in ERA in 1912 and 1913; pitched a no-hitter in 1920; inducted into the Hall of Fame in 1936

If you go to Bethesda, Maryland, you'll find **WALTER JOHNSON HIGH SCHOOL**. Walter lived in a house close by. The school's yearbook is called *The Windup*, and the student newspaper is named *The Pitch*. The names are all in tribute to one of the most amazing pitchers ever.

That's a record that still stands today and most likely will never be broken.

Another interesting thing about Walter was that he wasn't a mean pitcher. He wouldn't throw at hitters

intentionally to back them off the plate, which many pitchers do. Ty Cobb figured it out, so he would stand close to the plate whenever he faced Walter. Walter's pitches were just about the fastest anyone could throw, and Cobb was one of the few batters willing to take the risk of being hit. In addition to being a "kind pitcher," Walter never got into fights, didn't drink or curse, and never argued with the umpires.

Finally in 1924 something amazing happened. The Washington Senators, led by the great Walter Johnson, made it to the World Series against the New York Giants. How big a deal was that? President Calvin Coolidge was on hand to throw out the first pitch. Walter, of course, was on the mound for that first game, and he struck out 12 Giants. New York still won the game, but the Series wasn't over just yet.

The 1924 World Series came down to a dramatic seventh game in Washington. The Senators were trailing 3–1 in the eighth inning but tied the game. Guess who then came in to pitch in relief for Washington? Yup, the one and only Walter Johnson. He was 36 years old by then, and he was nearing the end of his career. He proceeded to pitch four scoreless innings. The Senators scored a run in the

AMERICAN LEAGUE
TRIPLE CROWN WINNER

1913
36 wins, 1.14 ERA, 243 strikeouts

1918
23 wins, 1.27 ERA, 162 strikeouts

1924
23 wins, 2.72 ERA, 158 strikeouts

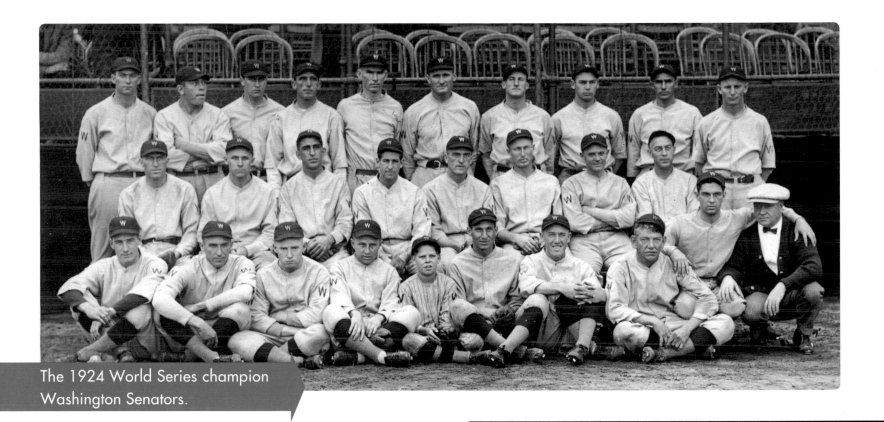

The 1924 World Series champion Washington Senators.

bottom of the twelfth inning to win the only World Series that the city of Washington has ever won.

Walter was not only one of the greatest pitchers; he was now a World Series champion. His career spanned 21 seasons, and when he finally retired in 1927, he had won 417 games—second only to Cy Young. His 3,508 strikeouts stood as a record for over a half a century before it was broken by Nolan Ryan in 1983. The only thing left for Walter was induction into the Baseball Hall of Fame. That came in 1936 when Cooperstown held its very first election. Walter got in, but Young didn't make it until the next year.

ERA stands for "earned run average," the average number of runs a pitcher gives up over the course of nine innings pitched. So let's say a pitcher worked six innings, and the opposing team scored two runs. Multiply 2 times 9 and then divide that number by 6 to get an ERA of 3.00.

$$\frac{\text{Earned Runs Allowed} \times 9}{\text{Innings Pitched}} = \text{ERA}$$

Walter Johnson once said, "You can't hit what you can't see." Okay, so he was exaggerating about the speed of his pitches. But not by much.

LOU GEHRIG

On July 4, 1939, there were over 62,000 fans in attendance at Yankee Stadium when Lou Gehrig stepped to the microphone to address the crowd. He uttered some of the most famous words in the history of sports. He said, "Today, I consider myself the luckiest man on the face of the earth." Lou was dying, and yet he thought of himself as being a lucky guy. After reading his story, you'll see why he felt that way.

Lou Gehrig was born in New York City in 1903. He was a terrific athlete who quickly gained attention. His high school baseball team traveled to Chicago to play another high school at Wrigley Field. Late in the game, Lou hit a grand slam clear out of the ballpark to help his school win. The fans were amazed. Home runs weren't as common back then. The next day in the newspaper, a reporter wrote: "Gehrig's blow would have made any big leaguer proud, yet it was walloped by a boy who hasn't yet started to shave." It's interesting that his grand slam got so much attention. As a big leaguer, Lou hit 23 grand slams. It's a record that still stands.

Lou then went to Columbia University, not for baseball, but on a football scholarship. He wound up playing both. A scout was so impressed by his ballplaying ability that the Yankees paid Lou a bonus of $1,500 to leave school and play professional baseball.

On June 2, 1925, the manager of the Yankees decided to start Lou at first base instead of the veteran, Wally Pipp. It started one of the most incredible streaks in sports history. Lou didn't miss a single game for the next 14 years! He played in 2,130 consecutive games. And it wasn't easy. At various times he had a broken thumb, a broken toe, and back problems. But Lou played through the pain. It was no surprise that his nickname became "the Iron Horse."

In 1925 Lou batted a respectable .295. Thirteen years later, his last full season, he also batted .295. Those 12 seasons in between were some of the best dozen years that any player has ever had. In fact, he never batted under .300.

In his first full season, 1926, Lou led the American League in triples and played in his first World Series.

Some thought Lou Gehrig's **RECORD FOR CONSECUTIVE GAMES PLAYED** would never be broken. It finally was, by **CAL RIPKEN JR.** of the Baltimore Orioles, in 1995.

When Lou Gehrig (L) and Babe Ruth were teammates, they hit more home runs between the two of them than just about every team in baseball.

Despite the fact that he hit .348 in the seven-game series, the Yankees lost to St. Louis 4 games to 3. But then came the magical year of 1927.

The core batting order for the 1927 New York Yankees was called "Murderer's Row." Lou batted fourth, also called the "cleanup position," which is normally reserved for the best slugger on the team. Batting third, just ahead of Lou, was none other than Babe Ruth. Is it any surprise that the 1927 Yankees are considered perhaps the greatest baseball team of all time?

That year Ruth set the record for home runs in a season at the time, with 60. Lou walloped another 47. The two of them had more homers than just about every entire team in baseball. But the home runs don't tell the whole story. Lou batted an amazing .373 in 1927, and he drove in an astonishing 175 runs. Thanks to the Babe and Lou, the Yankees rolled to the pennant, winning 110 games and losing just 44. And the World Series presented no problem. The Yankees swept Pittsburgh in four straight games. Lou was a World Series champion for the first time, and it wasn't the last.

What could the Yankees possibly do for an encore in 1928? Easy. They repeated as World Series champs. Lou batted .374 in the regular season and .545 in the World Series. It was another sweep, this time of the St. Louis Cardinals.

One of the best teams of all time, the 1927 New York Yankees.

The Yankees didn't get back to the World Series until 1932. One game that season really stands out. It was on June 3, and the Yankees were playing in Philadelphia. Lou came to bat in the first inning and hit a two-run homer. In the fourth inning, he hit another one. And the next inning, one more! No American League player had ever hit four home runs in one game, but in the seventh inning, Lou did it—his fourth home run in four straight at-bats! In the ninth inning, he almost hit his fifth, but it was caught. The Yankees beat the Philadelphia A's that day 20–13.

In the World Series that year, the Yanks played the Cubs. It was another four-game sweep.

Even though **LOU GEHRIG** and **BABE RUTH** were teammates for many years and two of the greatest players of all time, they weren't the best of friends. In fact, they stopped talking to each other for a while. They went for six years without even saying hello.

LOU "THE IRON HORSE" GEHRIG

THE 25 GREATEST BASEBALL PLAYERS OF ALL TIME

BORN: June 19, 1903

BIRTHPLACE: New York, NY

HEIGHT: 6'0" **WEIGHT:** 200 lbs.

TEAM: New York Yankees

BATS: Left   **THROWS:** Left

POSITION: First Base

NUMBER: 4

ROOKIE YEAR: 1923

CAREER BATTING AVERAGE: .340

CAREER HIGHLIGHTS: Voted the American League MVP in 1927 and 1936; voted to every All-Star Game from 1933 to 1939; won the American League Triple Crown for batting in 1934; uniform number (No. 4) was retired in 1939; inducted into the Hall of Fame in 1939

CAREER STATS:	TEAM	GAMES	BATTING AVERAGE	RBI	HR
Career Totals (1923–1939)	NYY	2,164	.340	1,995	493

By 1934, Ruth's skills were starting to fade, but Lou's were not. He had his best all-around season ever. Lou led the American League in batting average, home runs, and runs batted in (RBIs)—the Triple Crown. Winning the Triple Crown has only been accomplished nine times in American League history. But Lou's individual greatness wasn't enough to help the Yankees get to the World Series that year. And after the 1934 season, Ruth was released by the Yankees. The greatest one-two punch in baseball history, was…well, *history*.

The next season a pretty fair player joined the team as a rookie. His name was Joe DiMaggio. And, as crazy as it sounds, it was as if the Yankees never needed Ruth in the first place. Led by Lou and Joe DiMaggio, the Yankees proceeded to get to the next three World Series in a row. And they won all three!

But something happened in 1938. For the first time in ages, Lou batted under .300. And it wasn't just his batting average. His strength wasn't what it had been. The fly balls that used to be home runs now weren't leaving the park. And it got much worse in 1939. After playing just eight games and getting only four hits, Lou took himself out of the lineup. Remember, he hadn't missed a game since 1925! The amazing streak of playing in 2,130 straight games was now over. He never played another game.

Lou was not just slumping in 1938. He was sick—very sick. Doctors determined he had an awful disease with a very long name: amyotrophic lateral sclerosis. At the young age of 36, Lou was dying. Fans the world over were stunned and saddened. This deadly disease, which

Lou Gehrig gives his famous speech to a sold-out crowd at Yankee Stadium July 4, 1939.

In 1929 the Yankees wore uniform numbers for the first time. Babe Ruth wore No. 3, and Lou Gehrig No. 4. What was the reason they got those numbers? That's where they hit in the batting order.

claimed such a talented ballplayer, would become forever known as "Lou Gehrig's Disease."

The Yankees announced that on July 4, they would have Lou Gehrig Appreciation Day between games of a doubleheader against the Washington Senators. Several notable things happened that day. For one, the Yankees retired Lou's No. 4. It was the first time an athlete in any sport had his number retired.

Then there was the famous speech. "Today, I consider myself the luckiest man on the face of the earth," Lou began. He thanked his teammates, his manager, his opponents, and even the grounds keepers. He thanked his parents by saying that "when you have a father and a mother who work all their lives so you can have an education and build your body, it's a blessing." His last words in the speech were: "I close in saying that I may have had a rough break, but I have an awful lot to live for."

By the end, there wasn't a dry eye in Yankee Stadium, and Lou received a prolonged standing ovation. The next day in the newspaper, it was called "one of the most touching scenes ever witnessed on a ball field." Babe Ruth walked over and put his arm around him.

The usual waiting period was waived, and Lou was immediately inducted into the Baseball Hall of Fame. Lou had said he had a lot to live for, but he died two years later. Flags all over the city of New York and at ballparks around the country were flown at half-staff.

In 1999, Major League Baseball asked fans to vote for the All-Century Team. Guess who got the most votes of any player in history? None other than the Iron Horse himself, Lou Gehrig.

AMERICAN LEAGUE
TRIPLE CROWN WINNER

1934
49 HR, 165 RBIs,
.363 BA

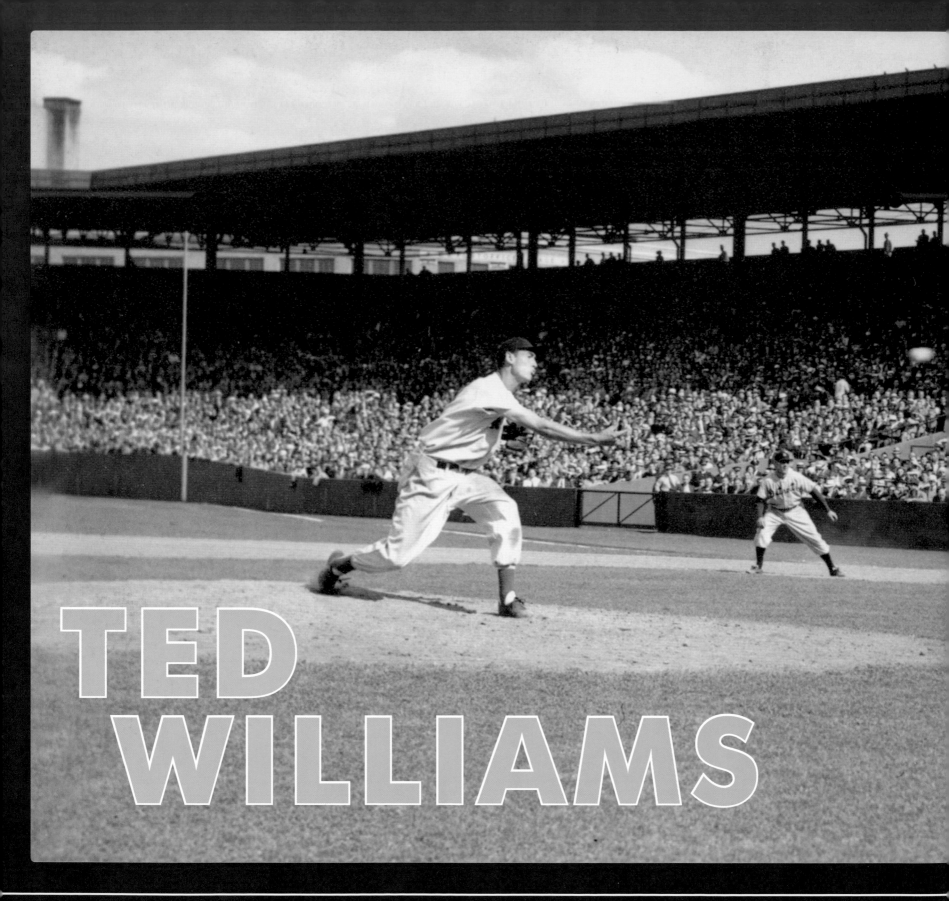

TED
WILLIAMS

I once heard Ted Williams say, "Hitting a baseball is the single most difficult act in sports because you have a round ball and a round bat and you have to hit it square." Most experts agree that nobody hit it square more often or better than Ted himself.

This one story may sum Ted up perfectly. It was the 1941 season, and coming into the last day, his batting average was .39955. That rounded up to .400. If Ted didn't play that day, he would have become the first hitter since 1930 to bat .400. But that wasn't in his nature. He felt that if he was going to be a .400 hitter, he'd have to do it for the entire season. So he played in both games of a doubleheader. He was up eight times and got six hits, finishing the season with a .406 average. That was Ted in a nutshell. It was also the last time any major leaguer batted .400.

Ted grew up in San Diego and quickly became a great baseball player. He led his high school team to the state championship and started his minor league baseball career at home in San Diego. After two years in San Diego and one year in Minneapolis, he was ready for the big time. He was just 20 years old, and he was now a rookie for the Boston Red Sox. What a year he had! He batted .327 and led the entire American League in runs batted in (RBIs) with 145. Back then baseball didn't have a Rookie of the Year Award. If it did, Ted surely would have won. But he did finish fourth in the voting for the Most Valuable Player (MVP) Award. Thus began an amazing career for the Red Sox left fielder that would span parts of four decades.

Ted's accomplishments were tremendous. He was voted the MVP of the American League twice, and he won two Triple Crowns, in 1942 and 1947. There is a gap of five years there. Why? Because after winning the Triple Crown in 1942, Ted had to go off to

Sunflower seeds are a popular food for the players! You can see many players chewing on sunflower seeds and spitting the shells all over the dugout during a game. It's a healthy (but messy) snack!

After missing three years due to military service, Ted Williams batted .342 and led the Red Sox to the 1946 World Series. They wound up losing to the St. Louis Cardinals in seven games. It was Ted's only World Series appearance. But his baseball and military careers were far from over. In the early 1950s, he missed two more seasons because of the Korean War. He flew 39 combat missions—some of them with John Glenn, who later became the first American to orbit Earth. So the great Ted Williams missed five full seasons because of two wars. When he retired in 1960, Ted Williams had hit 521 home runs. At the time he was third on the all-time list. Who knows what kind of stats he would have piled up if not for his time spent at war?

serve his country. He was a navy pilot during World War II. He then returned to baseball in 1946 and picked up right where he'd left off.

The Boston Red Sox had an amazing season in 1946. They wound up hosting the All-Star Game and the World Series in the same year. In the All-Star Game, Ted came to bat against pitcher Rip Sewell. Sewell threw what was called an "eephus pitch." It was basically the kind of high, slow toss you see in softball, but he threw it overhand, and major leaguers had trouble hitting it. In the All-Star Game, Ted came up against Sewell in the eighth inning. Ted was already 3 for 3 in the game, with a home run. He challenged Sewell to throw the eephus, and Sewell did. Ted swung and missed badly. Sewell motioned that he was going to throw him another one— but it was one too many. Ted proceeded to hit a three-run homer. It was the only time a player had ever hit a home run off Rip Sewell's eephus pitch.

Ted was a stubborn man both on and off the field. Since he was a lefty, when he came to bat, many teams would put on the "Williams shift." They would put three infielders between first and second base—and Ted would still try to

AMERICAN LEAGUE
TRIPLE CROWN WINNER

1947
32 HR, 114 RBIs, .343 BA

1942
36 HR, 137 RBIs, .356 BA

Ted Williams crosses home plate after hitting the final home run of his career on September 28, 1960.

pull the ball to the right side. The entire left side of the infield was being protected by just one fielder, so Ted could have easily gotten lots of hits by just going "the other way." But that wasn't his style.

Then there were the press and the fans. Ted would battle them all. He had a rocky relationship with sportswriters and would argue with them if he didn't like what they had written. Ted also got upset when he was occasionally booed by fans. So after his rookie year, Ted would never tip his cap to acknowledge the cheers of the fans.

Ted's last season was 1960, and his last game at Fenway Park was on September 28. In the eighth inning against Baltimore, Ted came up to bat for the last

Ted Williams batted .328 in 1958 at the age of 40. He was the **OLDEST PLAYER TO EVER WIN A BATTING TITLE.**

time in Boston—and wouldn't you know it? He hit a home run into the Red Sox bullpen in deep right-center field. He circled the bases as the fans rose to give him a standing ovation. Would this be the time that Ted would finally tip his cap to the fans—something he hadn't done for 20 years? The answer was no. He rounded the bases and headed to the dugout. No cap tipping. No curtain call. It was the last time he would ever bat in the major leagues.

Ted didn't disappear when his playing days were through.

500 HOME RUNS CLUB
Total Home Runs
521

Ted Williams won the **TRIPLE CROWN** twice in his career. The only other player to ever do that was Rogers Hornsby.

Ted Williams hits a home run against the Washington Senators.

He came back to manage the Washington Senators, and he was named Manager of the Year in 1969. He was inducted into the Baseball Hall of Fame in 1966, and in 1984 the Red Sox retired his No. 9.

In 1991, to commemorate the 50th anniversary of his batting .406, the Red Sox held Ted Williams Day at Fenway Park. After a brief speech, Ted pulled a Red Sox cap from his pocket and tipped it to the crowd. It was the first time he had done so in over half a century.

There was another incredible Ted Williams moment at Fenway Park. It was the 1999 All-Star Game, and Ted was brought to the pitcher's mound in a golf cart. He was in failing health as he threw out the first pitch. Again he waved his cap to the crowd and received a long standing ovation. All of the modern-day All-Stars gathered around Ted to shake his hand and talk to him about hitting. The major leaguers were in awe of Ted. They were in the presence of greatness and didn't want to leave.

Ted had always said that his goal in life was to be walking down the street and have a father say to his child, "Son, there goes the greatest hitter who ever lived." Well, it's been said millions of times now. When you list the greatest hitters of all time, the list begins with Ted Williams. Period.

TED "THE KID" WILLIAMS

THE 25 GREATEST BASEBALL PLAYERS OF ALL TIME

BORN: August 30, 1918

BIRTHPLACE: San Diego, CA

HEIGHT: 6'3" **WEIGHT:** 205 lbs.

TEAM: Boston Red Sox

BATS: Left

THROWS: Right

POSITION: Outfielder

ROOKIE YEAR: 1939

CAREER BATTING AVERAGE: .344

CAREER HIGHLIGHTS: Voted the Thomas A. Yawkey Red Sox MVP in 1941, 1946, 1949, and 1955; won the American League Triple Crown for batting in 1942 and 1947; voted the American League MVP in 1946 and 1949; voted to 19 All-Star Games during his career; uniform number (No. 9) was retired in 1960; inducted into the Hall of Fame in 1966

Ted Williams had a collection of nicknames, including "the Splendid Splinter," "the Kid," "the Thumper," and "Teddy Ballgame."

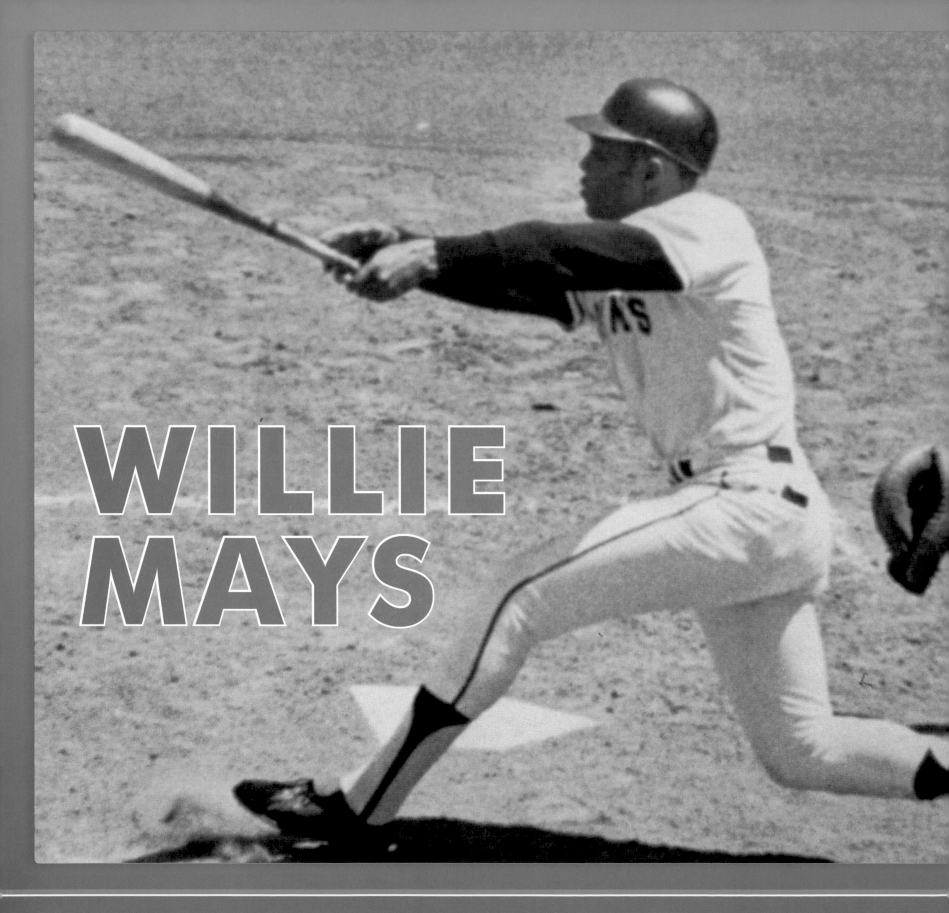

WILLIE
MAYS

In the 1950s there were three baseball teams in New York City, and they all had great center fielders: Mickey Mantle for the New York Yankees, Duke Snider for the Brooklyn Dodgers, and Willie Mays for the New York Giants. All three are in the Hall of Fame. But which one was the best? That was the subject of endless debates back in the day. Willie, Mickey, or the Duke? There was even a song written about them.

I grew up a Mickey Mantle fan, but I'll tell you the truth: I always thought that Willie Mays was the best of the three, and the simple reason was "he could do it all." Experts talk about five-tool players in baseball. Here are the tools: hit, hit with power, run, field, and throw. Willie was tops at all of them. He was also was exciting to watch. When you talk about the best all-around baseball players of all time, Willie has to be in the discussion.

Just look at his awards. He won them all: he was Rookie of the Year, Most Valuable Player (MVP), a 20-time All-Star selection, a 12-time Gold Glove winner for fielding, and best of all, World Series champion. Few players in the history of the game can boast all of that. But awards and stats are just awards and stats. Here's the story behind it all.

Willie was born in 1931 in the segregated South. He was the son of two athletic parents. His dad worked in a steel mill and played on the mill's baseball team, and his mom competed in track as a sprinter. They obviously passed on their athletic genes to young Willie. Willie's dad was teaching him to catch a ball before he could even walk.

His dad taught him about something else along the way—education. Willie could do it all, even back then. He was a terrific football and basketball player, but he wanted

WILLIE "THE SAY HEY KID" MAYS

BORN: May 6, 1931

BIRTHPLACE: Westfield, AL

HEIGHT: 5'11" **WEIGHT:** 180 lbs.

TEAMS: New York Giants, San Francisco Giants, New York Mets

BATS: Right **THROWS:** Right

POSITION: Outfield

ROOKIE YEAR: 1951

CAREER BATTING AVERAGE: .302

THE 25 GREATEST BASEBALL PLAYERS OF ALL TIME

CAREER HIGHLIGHTS: Voted to every All-Star Game from 1954 to 1973; voted the National League MVP in 1954 and 1965; won the Rawlings Gold Glove every year from 1957 to 1968; voted the All-Star MVP in 1963 and 1968; uniform number (No. 24) was retired in 1972; inducted into the Hall of Fame in 1979

to become a pro baseball player. His father was supportive, but he also made sure that Willie finished high school. Willie played part time in the Negro Leagues as a teenager, which allowed him to go to high school. And the very day he graduated from high school, he was signed to a pro contract by the New York Giants.

At the age of 18, it was off to the minor leagues. He didn't last long there. In his second minor league season, he was batting .477 in Minneapolis when the Giants called him up to the big leagues. There he was at the tender age of 20, a major leaguer. Surprisingly, it didn't start well. He struck out his first time at bat and didn't get a hit in three games in Philadelphia. He was 0 for 12.

Then the Giants returned home to the Polo Grounds, and the biggest crowd of the season showed up to see the heralded rookie. In his first at-bat in the first inning, against the great lefty Warren Spahn of the Milwaukee Braves, Willie hit a long home run to left field. It was the first of his 660 career homers.

In 1951 the Giants staged one of the greatest comebacks in baseball history to win the pennant. And right in the thick of things was the great rookie from Alabama, Willie Mays. Just like that, Willie Mays was in the World Series. He met up against a couple of Yankee stars. Joe DiMaggio was playing in his last World Series, and another famous rookie named Mickey Mantle was playing in his first fall classic. The Yankees won 4 games to 2, but

500 HOME RUNS CLUB

Total Home Runs

660

Willie wouldn't have to wait long to get another shot at a world championship.

First the Korean War intervened, and Willie went into the service for part of the 1952 season and all of 1953. What happened in 1954 was truly special. It featured perhaps the most incredible play in World Series history. Willie returned to baseball with a bang. He batted .345 to lead the National League in hitting. He was voted the league's MVP. And although he belted 41 homers, it was the triples that were truly special. He led the league in three-base hits—the first of three

times he did that in his career. Fans were thrilled at the sight of Willie tearing around the bases, often times with his cap flying off his head.

The Giants won the 1954 pennant and faced the powerful Cleveland Indians in the World Series. What

Willie Mays steals home plate against the Chicago Cubs.

happened in Game 1 at the Polo Grounds is the stuff of legend. The score was tied 2–2 in the eighth inning, with two Indians on base, when Vic Wertz of Cleveland hit a titanic blast to center field. Now center field in the Polo Grounds was vast. It went on and on. And so did Willie. Racing full speed, he somehow caught the ball way over 400 feet from home plate. Amazing. Willie then spun around and threw the ball back into the infield. Only one runner was able to advance, and neither wound up scoring. The Giants went on to win the game 5–2 in ten innings and never lost again, completing a sweep of the Indians. In just his second full season of major league baseball, Willie was a World Series champion.

Despite playing 19 more seasons with the Giants (both in New York and San Francisco) and with the New York Mets, Willie only got to two more World Series. He was on the losing end both times. But oh, the thrills he provided all those seasons. In one game, he hit four home runs. Nobody caught more fly balls in the history of baseball—and Willie did

Willie Mays makes his famous catch during the World Series against the Cleveland Indians.

This statue of Willie Mays is outside the Giants stadium in California.

Willie was a first ballot Hall of Famer, and his No. 24 was retired by the San Francisco Giants. In fact, No. 24 is everywhere at their ballpark. There's a bronze

3,000 HITS CLUB

Total Hits

3,283

statue of Willie that stands at the entrance to the Giants stadium. The address of the ballpark is 24 Willie Mays Plaza. The ballpark entrance is surrounded by 24 palm trees, and the height of the right field wall is 24 feet. By the way, every May 24 in San Francisco is Willie Mays Day, since Willie was born in May, and he wore No. 24.

Of course, the most famous picture of Willie, making that incredible catch in the 1954 World Series, captures him with his back to the infield so that the nice big "24" that adorns his uniform is exposed for all the world to see. That moment in time forever captures the spirit of Willie Mays, "the Say Hey Kid," perhaps the best all-around baseball player the game has ever seen.

it in style. He didn't catch fly balls the normal way. He used the "basket catch," where his glove would be near his waist and turned away from his body as he caught the ball. He finished playing in 1973 with a career batting average of .302, and he still holds the records for most home runs by a center fielder and most home runs hit in extra innings.

STAN MUSIAL

Just about all of the players in this book have nicknames. Stan Musial's might be the best of them all. He was simply "Stan the Man." And in baseball Stan was the man. The story of where he came from and what he became is the stuff of legends.

For starters he was born Stanislaus Musial in a small Pennsylvania town. He was a shy kid who got interested in baseball because a neighbor played semipro ball. So Stan picked up a broomstick and whacked a ball of tape around. He later said he could always get the bat on the ball, and as he went through life, he never stopped doing it. In fact, Stan became one of the greatest hitters of all time. But would you believe he started out as a pitcher?

The St. Louis Cardinals signed him at the age of 16 in the hopes that he would be a flame-throwing left-handed pitcher. He did throw the ball fast, but not very accurately. He would walk as many batters as he struck out. At one point his minor league manager said he'd never make it to the majors and recommended that he be released. As luck would have it, one of the outfielders got hurt, and Stan was put in the lineup. He batted .352. He would pitch some games and play the outfield in others. But he hurt his shoulder diving to make a catch one day, and his pitching career was basically over.

Stan was called up to the big leagues at the end of the 1941 season. He was just 20 years old. In the final 12 games of the 1941 season, the youngster hit .426! Nobody asked him to pitch again. He was now in the major leagues to stay.

Then came the 1942 season. Stan, at the age of 21, was the regular left fielder for the St. Louis Cardinals. Baseball didn't have a Rookie of the Year Award until 1947, when Jackie Robinson became the first winner, but if the award had existed in 1942, Stan would have won it. He batted .315 and led the Cardinals down the stretch of the pennant race. They got hot in September and beat out the Brooklyn Dodgers by two games. Suddenly, in his first full season in the majors, Stan found himself in the World Series against the mighty New York Yankees, who were led by Joe DiMaggio. After the Yankees won the first game, the Cards won the second. Stan's RBI single in the bottom of the eighth was the winning hit. And St. Louis didn't lose again. The Cardinals surprised the baseball world by winning the World Series in five games. Stan was now a World Series champion—and he wasn't finished.

The next season was simply amazing. By now Stan was a force, and he led the National League that year batting .357. He also led the league in doubles, triples, and several other offensive categories. In addition he got picked for his first All-Star Game. (He would go on to be selected for 24 All-Star Games.) He won the first of his three Most Valuable Player (MVP) Awards, as well. About the only thing he didn't do in 1943 was win the

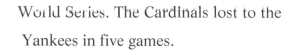

3,000 HITS CLUB
Total Hits
3,630

World Series. The Cardinals lost to the Yankees in five games.

But the next year, Stan led the Cards to another pennant and another World Series—his third straight. This time they beat the cross-town St. Louis Browns in six games as Stan batted over .300 for the Series.

What a start to a career—three full seasons, three World Series! Then something interfered: World War II. Stan was drafted in 1945 and spent a year repairing ships in the Navy in Hawaii. Without him, the Cards failed to win the pennant for the first time in four years.

Stan returned to baseball with a bang in 1946. He led the National League in just about everything except home runs and finished the year with an amazing .365 batting average. When the season ended, the Cards found themselves in a tie for first place with the Brooklyn Dodgers. It was the first time that ever happened, so a three-game playoff was held to decide who would go to the World Series. The Cardinals won two straight games and went on to beat Ted Williams and the Boston Red Sox in the 1946 World Series. Stan capped the year by winning his second MVP Award. But despite playing 17 more seasons for St. Louis, it was Stan's last World Series. The Cardinals never won another pennant with Stan.

No National League player has won the Triple Crown since Joe Medwick did it for the Cards in 1937. (To win

The baseball field Stan Musial played on as a teenager had a short left-field fence. That's because there were trolley tracks behind the wall. So Stan, a lefty hitter, would take aim at that short left-field wall. Thanks to those trolley tracks, Stan became a terrific opposite-field hitter.

the Triple Crown you have to lead the league in batting average, home runs, and RBIs.) In 1948 Stan batted .376 and drove in 131 runs. Those were his career bests, and they easily led the league. He also hit 39 homers—one shy of the Pirates' Ralph Kiner, who hit 40. But here's the fun part. Stan really did hit 40 homers that season, but one of them got rained out. The game was called off before it was an official game, so the homer didn't count. If it hadn't rained that day, Stan would have tied for the home-run lead and would have been declared the Triple Crown winner. Oh, well—as the saying goes, "You win some, you lose some, and some get rained out!"

So it went for Stan. He was a virtual hitting machine. And talk about consistency—he finished his career with 3,630 hits: 1,815 at home, and 1,815 on the road. Amazing. For 16 straight seasons, he batted over .300. Along the way, Stan won seven National League batting titles. He wasn't known as a slugger, yet over his career, he hit 475 home runs. And on May 2, 1954, he had one of the most incredible days in slugging history. The Cards played the New York Giants in a doubleheader in St. Louis. Stan went 6 for 8 in the two games. Five of the 6 hits were home runs. Nobody had ever hit five homers in a doubleheader before Stan Musial did it.

Stan received all the accolades a player can receive. His No. 6 was retired by the Cardinals, and there's a statue of

STAN "STAN THE MAN" MUSIAL

BORN: November 21, 1920
BIRTHPLACE: Donora, PA
HEIGHT: 6'0"   **WEIGHT:** 175 lbs.
TEAM: St. Louis Cardinals
BATS: Left   **THROWS:** Left
POSITION: Outfielder and first baseman
ROOKIE YEAR: 1941
CAREER BATTING AVERAGE: .331

THE 25 GREATEST BASEBALL PLAYERS OF ALL TIME

CAREER HIGHLIGHTS: Voted to 24 All-Star Games from 1943 to 1963; voted the National League MVP in 1943, 1946, and 1948; uniform number (No. 6) was retired in 1963; inducted into the Hall of Fame in 1969

him outside Busch Stadium. And, of course, he was elected to the Hall of Fame the first year his name was on the ballot.

Stan has commented that he is grateful for what baseball has done for him, giving him fame and fortune. He said, "I hope I've given nearly as much as I've gotten from it." Just ask anyone who ever saw him crouch at the left side of the plate and lash yet another hit to the outfield. Stan was definitely "the Man." Baseball may never see the likes of him again.

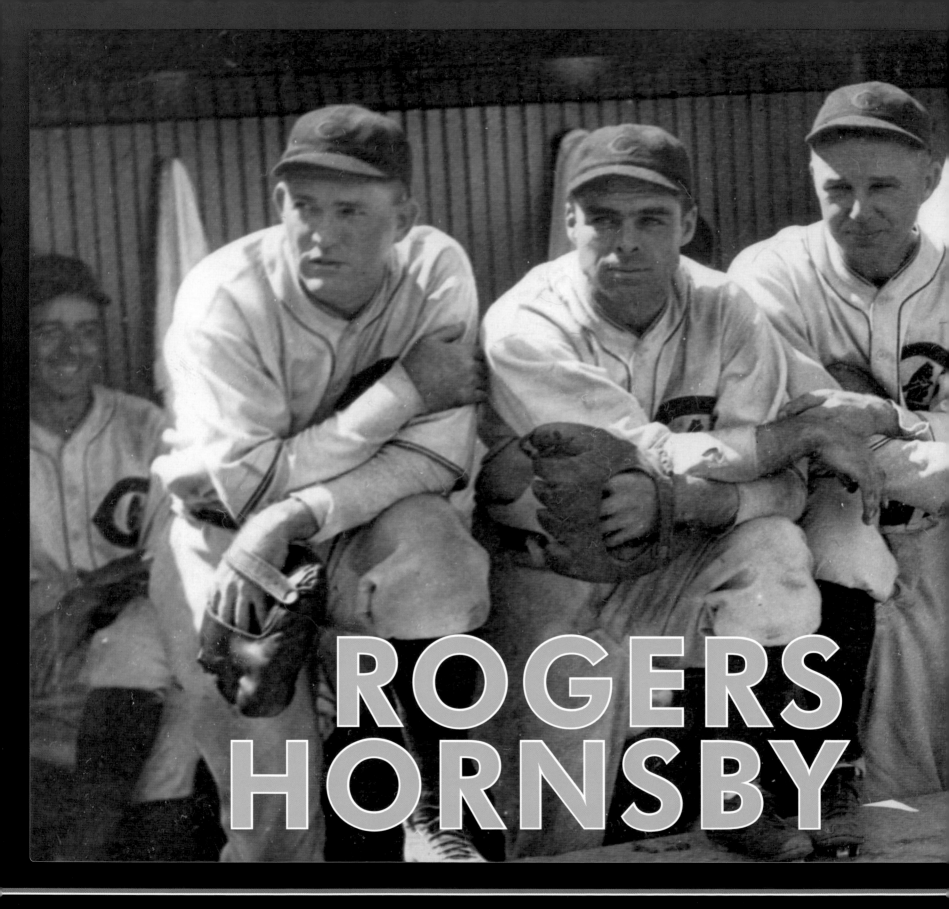

ROGERS
HORNSBY

How good a hitter was Rogers Hornsby? You can make an argument that he was one of the best…ever! Here's one little statistic for you: he finished his playing days with a .358 career batting average. No right-handed hitter in the history of baseball was better, and only Ty Cobb (a lefty hitter) had a higher lifetime average.

But statistics are just numbers. Here's a story that sums him up. Rogers always said that his first rule of thumb was to "get a good ball to hit." And boy, did he ever. It got to the point where one day, a rookie pitcher was on the mound pitching to Rogers. The pitcher was getting frustrated that all his pitches were being called balls. When he complained to the ump, the umpire responded, "Son, when you throw a strike, Mr. Hornsby will let you know."

Not much is known about Rogers's childhood. He was born in a small Texas town in 1896, and he loved to play baseball. Here's the ironic part: when he started out, he wasn't very good. He wasn't that big, wasn't a great fielder, and had trouble hitting. So his minor league career got off to a rocky start. Even when he got called up to the St. Louis Cardinals at the age of 19 in 1915, he wasn't so hot.

Then Rogers made a very important decision. He was going to get bigger and stronger. So he went to work on his uncle's farm in the off-season and showed up at spring training the following year having added 25 pounds of muscle. Obviously it worked. Suddenly he was a .300 hitter, and he stayed that way almost every season for the next two decades—except for when he batted over .400!

Here's another thing about Rogers Hornsby. He wasn't a very likeable guy. He was a tough competitor, and he was always getting into disagreements with the people who owned whatever team he was on. As a result, later in his career, he got traded a lot.

ROGERS "RAJAH" HORNSBY

BORN: April 27, 1896

BIRTHPLACE: Winters, TX

HEIGHT: 5'11" **WEIGHT:** 175 lbs.

TEAM: St. Louis Cardinals, New York Giants, Boston Braves, Chicago Cubs, St. Louis Browns

BATS: Right   **THROWS:** Right

POSITION: Second Base

ROOKIE YEAR: 1915

CAREER BATTING AVERAGE: .358

THE 25 GREATEST BASEBALL PLAYERS OF ALL TIME

CAREER HIGHLIGHTS: Won the National League Triple Crown for batting in 1922 and 1925; voted the National League MVP in 1925 and 1929; holds the second-highest all-time career batting average (.358); inducted into the Hall of Fame in 1942

Rogers Hornsby was unique: not only was he a batting champ and player/manager, but he didn't smoke and he also didn't drink. He wouldn't even drink coffee. In addition to that, he wouldn't watch movies or read! He thought those activities would be harmful to his batting eye. Imagine that.

Now, you would think with a personality like that, he would get into fights during games, but it didn't happen. In fact, he never even argued with the umpires. He went through his entire career without getting thrown out of a single game. Pretty amazing when you consider his nature.

The 1920s started with Rogers winning the National League batting title. He batted an incredible .397. But that was just the beginning. He won the batting crown for six consecutive seasons. In 1921 he almost did it all. Two more hits and he would have batted a magical .400. He hit 21 homers, as well, which was two home runs shy of winning the Triple Crown. And he would do even better in 1922 with truly one of the most amazing seasons that any batter has ever had.

In 1922 Rogers hit a cool .401. Remember those 21 homers the previous year? He doubled it in 1922 by hitting 42 of them. To top it off, he drove in a staggering 152 runs. He won the 1922 Triple Crown, and in doing so, he batted over .400 and hit at least 40 home runs. Nobody had ever done that in the same season, and nobody has done it since!

In 1924 he batted an even more incredible .424. Nobody ever had a higher batting average in the modern era. The next year, in 1925, he added something else to his resume: the title of manager. Yep, he was the star player and the manager of the St. Louis Cardinals at the same time. Even though the Cards finished in fourth place, he won another Triple Crown and topped it off with the first of his two Most Valuable Player (MVP) Awards.

Have you noticed I haven't mentioned the World Series anywhere? Despite all of his amazing feats, the Cardinals hadn't made it to the World Series with him. But that all changed in 1926. Again Rogers was the manager, and that took its toll on his batting average. He slipped all the way down to .317. That's pretty good for most players, but it wasn't too terrific for Rogers Hornsby. Despite the slippage, the Cardinals made it to the 1926 World Series, where they faced Babe Ruth, Lou Gehrig, and the great New York Yankees.

It all came down to a seventh game at Yankee Stadium. The Cardinals were leading 3–2 in the bottom of the ninth. Ruth walked with two outs, representing the potential tying run. Then he tried to steal second base, but he was thrown out. It was the only time a World Series ever ended with a player caught stealing. It also meant that Rogers Hornsby was now a World Series champion for the one and only time in his marvelous career.

Despite the Cardinals' success in 1926, Rogers continued to argue

NATIONAL LEAGUE
TRIPLE CROWN WINNER

1922
42 HR, 152 RBIs,
.401 BA

1925
39 HR, 143 RBIs,
.403 BA

with the owner of the team. He thought the owner was cheap. After they won the World Series, Rogers demanded a three-year contract for $50,000 a year. The owner not only refused, he traded Rogers to the New York Giants. But Rogers got into more arguments with management there and got traded the next year to the Boston Braves. The year after that, he got traded to the Chicago Cubs. The Cubs thought so much of Rogers that they traded five players to the Braves, plus $200,000 to get him. Rogers did help the Cubs get to the World Series in 1929, but this time he came up on the losing side as the surprising Philadelphia Athletics won in five games.

That was Rogers's last full season in the major leagues. He made the Hall of Fame the first time his name was on the ballot, in 1942. When all said and done, Rogers Hornsby is definitely considered one of the giants of the game.

FAST FACT

The home-plate umpire is considered the "lead" umpire. He's responsible for calling the pitches (whether it's a strike or a ball), and the other umpires rely on him for making all the final calls for plays on the field.

HONUS WAGNER

So what baseball card is the most valuable? Babe Ruth? Mickey Mantle? Nope. It's Honus Wagner. One of his cards once sold for $2.8 million—and it wasn't because he was the best player. In 1909 a tobacco company put out a series of cards, one of which featured him. Honus Wagner got upset about it. Some thought it was because he didn't smoke and didn't want to present that image to kids. Others thought the real reason was that he wanted to be paid to have his picture on a card. Whatever the reason, he demanded that the company stop distributing his cards, so it's believed there are only 60 or so of those cards in existence. If the card is in great condition, it's worth a ton of money. But that's just a small part of the Honus Wagner legacy.

Honus is considered by many to be the best shortstop to ever play the game. He could do it all—hit, drive in runs, and steal bases. Defensively, he was without competition. Honus was the first player to steal second, third, and home in the same inning. He did it four times in his career. He was also the first player to ever have his own model Louisville Slugger autographed bat.

Honus Wagner was born before 1900 in a suburb of Pittsburgh. He was one of nine kids. (Hey, the Wagner kids could have fielded their own baseball team!) Growing up he worked in coal mines, steel mills, and even his brother's barber shop. But most of all, he and his brothers liked to play baseball. When he started out, he played a few different positions, both infield and outfield. In fact, he didn't settle in as a shortstop until his sixth year in the major leagues. And what a shortstop he was! He was described as being bowlegged with long limbs. It was said that he was like an octopus scooping up ground balls and throwing them to first. Nobody could do it better. There was even a story that while playing shortstop during a game, he was reaching into his back pocket with his glove hand to get something. Just then the ball was hit to him, so he grabbed it with his bare hand and threw the runner out at first. He did it literally with one hand behind his back.

Honus played almost his entire career for his hometown Pittsburgh Pirates. That was where he got the nickname "the Flying Dutchman" for his speed on the base paths. In fact, he led the National League in stolen bases five times. His sixth season in a Pirate uniform, 1903, was one for the record books. Honus won the batting title as the Pirates captured the National League pennant. The owner of the Pirates, a man named Barney Dreyfuss, then had an idea. He challenged the winner of the American League, the Boston Americans, with their great pitcher, Cy Young, to a best-of-nine championship series. Thus the very first World Series was born.

Honus didn't fare well in the first fall classic, batting just .222, and the Pirates lost to the Americans 5 games to 3. It really bothered Honus that he had played so poorly. He had won the National League batting championship for the second time, but he felt that by not playing well in the World Series, he wasn't a clutch performer.

But he won the batting title again in 1904, and then did it for four straight years, from 1906 through 1909. But he almost didn't make it that far. After the 1907 season, he threatened to retire. His team's owner would have none of that. He offered Honus a whopping $10,000 to come back in 1908. That made him the highest-paid player in all of baseball. And Honus proved he was worth it. In 1908 he very nearly won the Triple Crown. He led the National League in hitting and runs batted in (RBIs). He also hit 10 home runs, but he fell two shy of the league lead, thus missing that Triple Crown.

The following year, 1909, he got another crack at the World Series. The Pirates won an amazing 110 games, and Honus led the league in virtually every statistical category. What a World Series matchup it was: the Pittsburgh Pirates against the Detroit Tigers; Honus Wagner versus Ty Cobb, the two premier hitters of their day. In fact, it was the first time that the batting champs of both leagues squared off against each other in the World Series.

This time Honus didn't disappoint. Despite being 35 years old, while Cobb was just 22, Wagner prevailed. He not only hit .333 for the Series, but the Flying Dutchman stole a record six bases. It all came down to a seventh game. Honus drove in two runs in an 8–0 Pirates rout. The city

3,000 HITS CLUB
Total Hits
3,415

of Pittsburgh had won its first world championship.

But Honus's career was far from over. He played eight more seasons, and even though he never got back to the World Series, he won yet another batting title and continued to do some amazing things. At the age of 40, he got his 3,000th career hit. He was just the second player to ever do that. And when he hit a grand slam at the age of 41, he was the oldest modern player to ever accomplish that feat. It was an inside-the-park homer, so he had to motor all the way around the bases to do it. It was a record that stood for 70 years.

When he finally retired from baseball in 1917, Honus was the all-time hits leader in National League history—a record that has since been broken. And as you can imagine, he had his share of honors. His No. 33 was retired by the Pirates, but that was the number he wore as a coach after he finished playing. When Honus played baseball, there were no uniform numbers.

When the Hall of Fame opened its doors in 1936, Honus was in the very first class to be inducted, along with Babe Ruth, Walter Johnson, Ty Cobb, and Christy Mathewson. In fact, Honus received the same number of votes as the great Babe Ruth!

Various votes have been taken over the years to select the greatest baseball players of all time, and one result

is virtually unanimous. When it comes to the best all-around shortstop to ever play the game of baseball, the hands-down winner is Honus Wagner.

HONUS "THE FLYING DUTCHMAN" WAGNER

THE **25** GREATEST BASEBALL PLAYERS OF ALL TIME

BORN: February 24, 1874

BIRTHPLACE: Chartiers, PA

HEIGHT: 5'11" **WEIGHT:** 200 lbs.

TEAM: Louisville Colonels, Pittsburgh Pirates

BATS: Right **THROWS:** Right

POSITION: Shortstop

ROOKIE YEAR: 1897

CAREER BATTING AVERAGE: .327

CAREER HIGHLIGHTS: First player to steal second base, third base, and home in the same inning; first player to have an autographed model Louisville Slugger bat with his name on it; led the National League in stolen bases five times; led the National League in batting average six times; inducted into the Hall of Fame in 1936; uniform number (No. 33) was retired in 1956

There's a statue of Honus Wagner outside the Pirates ballpark.

MICKEY
MANTLE

When I was a kid, Mickey Mantle was my idol. Heck, he was *everyone's* hero: a handsome, speedy, switch-hitting slugger who was in the World Series virtually every year. What kid wouldn't want "the Mick" as his hero? Long home runs are called "tape-measure homers" because of Mickey. He once hit a home run so far in Washington that somebody took a tape measure to figure out how long it went. Now you would think somebody with so much talent had it made from the very beginning. Not true. Mickey wanted to quit baseball early in his career. But let's start when he was a kid.

As soon as he could swing a bat and throw a ball, Mickey's dad would play baseball with him. His father was a miner who had played semipro baseball. In fact, his dad loved baseball so much that he named Mickey after Hall of Fame catcher Mickey Cochrane. Mickey's father and grandfather pitched to him every day in the yard of their home in Commerce, Oklahoma. They taught Mickey to swing from both sides of the plate, so he became a switch-hitter at a very young age.

As for his power—Mickey would work in the lead mines along with his father, and one of his jobs was to smash rocks with a sledgehammer. That's how he built up such amazing strength in his wrists, arms, and shoulders.

Mickey was an incredible athlete. In high school he played baseball, football, and basketball. When he was 16 years old, a major league scout came to see one of his baseball games. That day Mickey hit one home run as a righty and one as a lefty. The homers went over the fence and into a river outside the ballpark. The scout

Mickey Mantle played **BASEBALL, FOOTBALL, AND BASKETBALL** in high school. Once during football practice, he suffered an injury that nearly cost him his entire career. He was accidentally kicked in the shin, and the bone got infected. At one point doctors wanted to cut off his leg. But he was given a new miracle drug called penicillin, and his leg was saved.

couldn't believe that somebody so young was so talented. He promised to return the day that Mickey graduated high school to sign him to a contract. And he did. And that's how Mickey Mantle became the property of the New York Yankees.

Mickey played one full season at the minor league C level before he was invited to spring training with the world-champion New York Yankees in 1951. He so impressed manager Casey Stengel with his speed and power that he made the big-league club at the age of just 19. Nobody had ever jumped from C ball directly to the Yankees.

Mickey was given No. 6, which was pressure enough. The Yankees who had worn Nos. 3, 4, and 5 were all Hall of Famers, and they are all among the 25 players in this book: Babe Ruth, Lou Gehrig, and Joe DiMaggio. Now this 19-year-old kid was being brought up to the two-time defending champs to play right field. The Yankees already had a center fielder at the time—Joe DiMaggio.

That's when the trouble started. Mickey went into a slump. For the first time in his life, he was having trouble hitting. By the summer,

Mickey Mantle (R) and the great Joe DiMaggio get ready for an exhibition game in Mickey's rookie year.

Stengel sent him down to the minor leagues. Mickey called his dad and told him he didn't think he could play baseball anymore. So his dad drove from Oklahoma to Kansas City to see his son. Mickey expected some kind words of comfort. Instead his dad started packing up Mickey's clothes. He told his son that he thought he had raised a man, not a coward and a quitter. And he told Mickey that he could come back and work in the Oklahoma mines with him.

Mickey Mantle hits his 500th home run on May 14, 1967, at Yankee Stadium.

Talk about a wake-up call! The Mick didn't quit. He finally found his stroke, and before long, he was back in the major leagues—for good! He was given No. 7 instead of No. 6, to take some of the pressure off of him. The Mick went on to become the most famous No. 7 in the history of sports, and at the end of that season, the Yankees beat the Giants in the World Series.

By the following year, DiMaggio had retired, and now 20-year-old Mickey was the center fielder for the Yankees. And what an amazing run of success both he and the Yankees had! For 13 seasons from 1952 to 1964, the Yankees, led by their incredible center fielder, were in the World Series 11 times.

Mickey's first full season in 1952 set the tone. He batted

500 HOME RUNS CLUB
Total Home Runs
536

Mickey Mantle hit his first "tape-measure" home run in Washington. It was measured at 565 feet. He once hit a home run in Detroit that was estimated at 643 feet (but was not officially measured at the time)! And **HE VERY NEARLY HIT A HOME RUN OUT OF YANKEE STADIUM**—a feat that was never accomplished by any player.

MICKEY "THE MICK" MANTLE

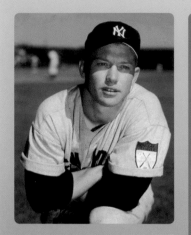

BORN: October 20, 1931

BIRTHPLACE: Spavinaw, OK

HEIGHT: 5'11" **WEIGHT:** 198 lbs.

TEAM: New York Yankees

BATS: Switch

THROWS: Right

POSITION: Outfielder

ROOKIE YEAR: 1951

CAREER BATTING AVERAGE: .298

THE 25 GREATEST BASEBALL PLAYERS OF ALL TIME

CAREER HIGHLIGHTS: Voted to every All-Star Game from 1952 to 1965 and 1967 and 1968; voted the American League MVP in 1956, 1957, and 1962; won the American League Triple Crown for batting in 1956; won the Rawlings Gold Glove in 1962; uniform number (No. 7) was retired in 1969; inducted into the Hall of Fame in 1974

Fans attempt to get Mickey Mantle's autograph before an exhibition game in San Juan.

over .300, hit 23 homers, and drove in 87 runs. However, the only category in which he led the league was strikeouts, which he did five times overall. He also led the league in walks five times. He would joke that between all his walks and strikeouts, he totaled two complete seasons in which he never had to run of out of the batter's box. In fact, it was either all or nothing for Mickey. Over the course of his career, he either hit a homer, struck out, or walked nearly half of his times up to bat.

Mickey won the World Series in his first three seasons with the Yankees. Then in 1956 he had his best season of all, winning the Triple Crown. He batted .353, hit 52 homers, and drove in 130 runs. He won another World Series that year and also won the first of his three Most Valuable

Player (MVP) Awards. And for a while that year many fans had thought Mickey would beat Babe Ruth's record of 60 homers in a season.

He challenged the home-run record again in 1961, when he and Roger Maris staged the greatest home-run race between teammates in baseball history. When it ended, Maris had broken the Babe's record by hitting 61. The Mick, who suffered an injury late in the season, came in second with 54.

In his 18-year career, Mickey Mantle played in **12 WORLD SERIES!**

Mickey's awards and records go on and on. He won the World Series seven times, and his record of 18 World Series home runs still stands today. He was a 16-time All-Star and had his No. 7 retired by the Yankees. Naturally, he was elected to the Baseball Hall of Fame the first year he was eligible.

One of my most prized possessions is an autographed baseball signed by Mickey. It reads, "To Len, thanks a lot. Mickey Mantle." I never got to ask him what he was thanking me for. Maybe it was for caring so much about him, which really wasn't very hard to do. I couldn't be happier to include Mickey in my book of the greatest baseball players of all time. My hero!

Fans rush to congratulate Mickey Mantle as he rounds the bases after hitting the home run to win a game against the Chicago White Sox.

PETE
ROSE

The objective of every batter who has ever played baseball is to simply get a hit. And in the history of baseball, no player has ever gotten more hits than Pete Rose. He is also the all-time leader in games played and times at bat. And yet he is not in the Hall of Fame. He is the only retired player in this book who is not in Cooperstown—and it has nothing to do with his playing ability.

Pete grew up in Cincinnati, Ohio, but he wasn't exactly a can't-miss prospect. When he graduated from high school in 1960, he signed with his hometown team for a "whopping" $7,000. If he got to the major leagues and stayed there for a year, he would get $500 more. It was the best deal the Cincinnati Reds ever made!

Pete headed to the minor leagues and immediately showed his stuff. He was a switch-hitter who batted over .300, and after only two years in the minors, he got his chance with Cincinnati. Pete was immediately noticed. When he walked, he wouldn't trot to first base like all the other players. He would run. Some thought he was brash and that he was being a hot dog. Others said it just showed how he was hustling all the time. He got tagged with the nickname "Charlie Hustle," and the name stuck. Also at the time, players would slide feet-first into the bases. Not Pete. He popularized the headfirst slide. He made so much of an impression that he won the National League Rookie of the Year Award in 1963. It was the first of many honors he would receive.

Throughout the rest of the 1960s, you could count on three things: Pete would bat over .300, he'd collect at least 200 hits most years, and he would often switch positions. He started as a second baseman, but by the time he ended his career, he had been voted to 17 All-Star Games at five different positions: left field, right field, first base, second base, and third base.

But even though Pete was a star player, the Reds never made it to the postseason in the 1960s. That all changed in 1970. The Cincinnati Reds moved into a new stadium that year.

The new Riverfront Stadium hosted the 1970 All-Star Game. And it featured one of the most memorable plays in All-Star history, which involved Charlie Hustle.

The game was tied in the twelfth inning when Pete scored the winning run for the National League. But it wasn't just an ordinary run. Instead of sliding into home plate headfirst, Pete barreled over Cleveland catcher Ray Fosse. The All-Star Game is in many respects an exhibition game, but Pete didn't treat it that way. His hustle won the game for the National League. Unfortunately Fosse injured his shoulder on the play, and he was never the same player again.

That same year the Reds finally made it to the postseason. It was the first of eight trips that Pete made to the playoffs. Although the Reds lost the 1970 World Series to the Baltimore Orioles, it was their first year of being a powerhouse team that became known as "the Big Red Machine." The team consisted of many stars, including catcher Johnny Bench, who is also featured in this book. But Pete was the guy who jump-started the

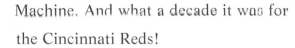

3,000 HITS CLUB
Total Hits
4,256

Machine. And what a decade it was for the Cincinnati Reds!

Some of the highlights: The Reds made it back to the World Series in 1972, but lost in a seven-game series to the Oakland A's. In 1973 the Reds took on the Mets in the National League Championship Series. Even though the Mets won, Pete dominated the series. He batted .381 and hit a couple of big home runs. He also got into a bench-clearing brawl with Mets shortstop Bud Harrelson. That was Pete—in the middle of everything.

Then came 1975. The Reds won 108 games as Pete led the National League with 112 runs scored. That set the stage for one of the most thrilling and dramatic World Series of all time. It came down to a seventh game against the Red Sox at Fenway Park in Boston. The score was tied at 3 when the Reds scored a run in the top of the ninth to win the Series. Pete was a champion for the first time. He was also voted World Series Most Valuable Player (MVP).

The following year the Reds won again when they swept the Yankees in the World Series. Pete won three World Series in all, the last in 1980 as a member of the Philadelphia Phillies.

During the 1978 season, Pete made a serious run at one of the most hallowed records in baseball: Joe DiMaggio's record of getting a hit in 56 consecutive games. Pete

In 1978 Pete Rose had a hit in each of 44 consecutive games!

would tie the National League record of 44 straight, but he failed to get a hit the next game, and his amazing streak ended. However, he still had one more incredible record to chase.

It was the night of September 11, 1985. Pete was now back with Cincinnati after playing for both Philadelphia and Montreal. He was the player/manager of the Reds. Pete was tied with the great Ty Cobb for the most hits in major league history. Ironically, exactly 57 years ago that day, Cobb had played his last game. Pete singled to left field against the San Diego Padres, and the crowd went wild. The game came to a halt as his teammates raced from the dugout to hug him. Pete was in tears as he waved to the fans. The owner of the Reds had a present for Pete: a red Corvette with the license plate PR 4192. It was driven in from the outfield. Pete now stood alone on the top of the mountain: 4,192 hits. He would get 64 more before he retired the following season.

When Pete retired in 1986, he held all sorts of records that still stand today. He also received just about every baseball award possible. And yet he is not in the Hall of Fame. Here's the reason. While he was the manager of the Reds, he placed bets on baseball games. He said he only bet on his team to win, but it didn't matter. It's against the rules of baseball to bet. In 1989 Pete was banned

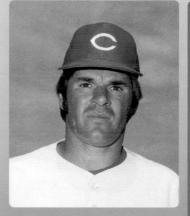

PETE "CHARLIE HUSTLE" ROSE

BORN: April 14, 1941
BIRTHPLACE: Cincinnati, OH
HEIGHT: 5'11" **WEIGHT:** 200 lbs.
TEAMS: Cincinnati Reds, Philadelphia Phillies, Montreal Expos
BATS: Switch **THROWS:** Right
POSITION: First Base
ROOKIE YEAR: 1963
CAREER BATTING AVERAGE: .303

THE 25 GREATEST BASEBALL PLAYERS OF ALL TIME

CAREER HIGHLIGHTS: Voted the National League Rookie of the Year in 1963; voted to 17 All-Star Games from 1965 to 1985; won the Rawlings Gold Glove in 1969 and 1970; voted the National League MVP in 1973; won the Silver Slugger in 1981; voted the World Series MVP in 1975

from baseball. That meant he couldn't work for any team or even show up for team promotions. That's why his No. 14 was never officially retired by the Reds. Most of all, it meant he was not eligible for the Baseball Hall of Fame.

Baseball experts have debated for years whether or not this is fair. But the rules are the rules. And even though Pete Rose is clearly one of the best players to ever play the game, you will not find his plaque in Cooperstown.

JOSH
GIBSON

There is only one player in this book who never played in the major leagues, but that didn't stop him from making it to the Baseball Hall of Fame. His name is Josh Gibson. He was otherwise known as "the Black Babe Ruth."

There is one reason, and one reason alone, that Josh never played in the majors. It's because of the color of his skin. Before 1947, Major League Baseball discriminated against African American players and wouldn't let them play in the big leagues. That finally ended in April 1947, when Jackie Robinson broke the "color barrier" for the Brooklyn Dodgers. It came too late for Josh Gibson by a matter of months.

Josh was born in Georgia, but his family moved to Pittsburgh when he was a boy. His father worked in the steel mills. Josh was big, strong, and fast. He won several awards at local track meets. But baseball was his first love. He stood 6 feet, 1 inch and weighed 210 pounds. Because of his solid build, he wound up being a catcher. But defense wasn't his strength—offense was. He went from the sandlots of Pittsburgh to become the greatest slugger in the history of the Negro Leagues.

The Negro Leagues were formed as far back as the 1920s and lasted well into the 1950s. That was the league where African American baseball players could compete. Some of the most successful teams were the Pittsburgh Crawfords, the Homestead (Pennsylvania) Grays, the Kansas City Monarchs, and the Indianapolis Clowns.

The accurate history of the Negro Leagues, like its actual box scores, is hard to come by. So much of what is known about Josh Gibson is the stuff of legend. For example, in one game at Yankee Stadium, it was said that he hit a home run clear out of the ballpark. Nobody had ever done that—not even Babe Ruth. Nobody knows if it's really true. It is known that he hit one of the longest home runs ever hit in "the House that Ruth Built." He drove the ball deep into the left-field bullpen, over 500 feet from home plate.

JOSH GIBSON

BORN: December 21, 1911

BIRTHPLACE: Buena Vista, GA

HEIGHT: 6'1" **WEIGHT:** 210 lbs.

TEAMS: Homestead Grays, Pittsburgh Crawfords

BATS: Right **THROWS:** Right

POSITION: Catcher

ROOKIE YEAR: 1929

CAREER BATTING AVERAGE: .354

THE 25 GREATEST BASEBALL PLAYERS OF ALL TIME

CAREER HIGHLIGHTS: Estimated to have hit more than 900 home runs during his 17-season career; led the Negro National League in home runs for 10 consecutive years; inducted into the Hall of Fame in 1972

JOSH GIBSON is said to have hit such an amazing clout at Comiskey Park in Chicago that he **KNOCKED A SPEAKER OFF THE ROOF** in center field.

We don't really know for sure how many home runs Josh hit. Some claim it was nearly 800. Others say it was over 900, which would make him the greatest home-run hitter who ever lived. The reason we don't know is that he didn't just play in Negro League games. During the off season he would barnstorm with All-Star teams around the country, and he would also play in Mexico and in the Caribbean. That's why his homer totals grew to such huge proportions. One year, playing for a wide variety of teams, he is said to have hit 84 home runs, which, of course, would be the all-time record if he had done it during one season in the big leagues.

It's believed that Josh won several Negro League home-run and batting titles. In fact, while catching for the Homestead Grays, Josh's team won nine consecutive Negro League pennants. In addition he appeared in numerous Negro League All-Star Games and Negro World Series. But since his statistics aren't really "official," the numbers don't tell the whole story of Josh. What truly reveals the nature of his greatness are the stories that other people tell about him. Here are some examples.

It is said that Josh was the only player, other than Mickey Mantle, to have hit a baseball clear out of Griffith Stadium in Washington, DC. Mantle's homer there gave birth to the phrase "tape-measure homer."

Walter Johnson, one of the all-time great pitchers once said that any big-league team would want to have Josh Gibson. Johnson said, "He can do everything. He hits the ball a mile. He catches so easy he may as well be in a rocking chair. Throws like a rifle."

Josh Gibson practices his swing before a game.

Three other players in this book began their careers in the Negro Leagues: **HANK AARON, WILLIE MAYS,** and **JACKIE ROBINSON.**

"There is a catcher that any big league club would love. His name is Gibson... he can do everything."

—WALTER JOHNSON

Monte Irvin was a star outfielder for the New York Giants in the early 1950s. He had also played in the Negro Leagues. He said that Josh was the greatest hitter he had ever seen, black or white! And Irvin played with both Willie Mays and Hank Aaron.

This may be one of the funniest legends ever told about Josh Gibson: As the story goes, his team was trailing by one run in the bottom of the ninth in Pittsburgh. With two outs and a runner on base, Josh belted such a long, towering home run that it disappeared from sight, winning the game. The next day the same two teams played in Philadelphia. As the teams were getting ready for the game, a baseball came falling out of the sky. It was caught by a Philadelphia outfielder. The umpire then yelled at Josh, "You're out. In Pittsburgh, yesterday!"

Such was the legend of Josh Gibson.

Josh died far too young—he was only 35 when he passed away from a stroke. Ironically he left this earth just three months before Jackie Robinson broke the color barrier.

Twenty-five years after his death, Josh Gibson, having never played in the majors, was nevertheless inducted into the Baseball Hall of Fame. He may have been the greatest slugger of them all. The sad truth is that we'll never know for sure.

BOB
FELLER

So here's how you know a pitcher is really special and has a great fastball. He's got more than one nickname, like "Rapid" and "Bullet." Rapid, of course, goes very nicely with Robert. And Bullet works just as well with Bob. Bob Feller was a pitching phenom, and his story is about as American as it gets. It all started on a farm in Iowa, and his journey took him through baseball greatness, into World War II, and on a little trip to the charming upstate town of Cooperstown, New York, and induction into the Baseball Hall of Fame.

As a kid Bob would play catch with his dad on their farm and spend hours throwing a baseball against the wall of their hog barn. That's where he developed his righty "windmill" delivery with a high leg kick. All of the chores he had to perform, like milking cows and picking corn, built up the strength in his arm. It was no surprise that he became a pitcher on his high school team.

The Cleveland Indians noticed Bob, and they signed him to a "huge contract." It was for $1 and an autographed baseball. The Indians knew they had someone special. How special? He never pitched a day in the minor leagues. During summer vacation after his junior year in high school, while all of his friends were working on their farms, Bob took a little trip…to pitch for the Cleveland Indians!

The very first time he pitched for the Indians, it was in an exhibition game against the St. Louis Cardinals. Bob was just 17 years old. He pitched only three innings, yet he struck out eight Cards. The high schooler mowed down major leaguers with ease. The next month he made his first major league start against the St. Louis Browns and struck out 15 batters. He was just getting warmed up. In September he struck out 17 Philadelphia A's to tie the major league record of the great Dizzy Dean.

Talk about bursting onto the scene. Bob had pitched only 62 innings, but he had recorded 76 strikeouts. He was the talk of baseball, so much so that the following spring, when he was just 18 years old, he appeared on the cover of *Time* magazine—and he had yet to finish high school! That happened a couple of months later, and it was such a big deal that NBC broadcast his high school graduation live on the radio from coast to coast. Imagine that!

By the 1938 season, Bob was all of 19 years old, and his career really took off. On the last day of the season, the Indians were playing Detroit. A big crowd turned out in Cleveland to see Hank Greenberg of the Tigers. Greenberg

Just for fun in 1940, in a park in Chicago, Bob Feller **RACED HIS PITCHING SPEED VERSUS A MOTORCYCLE**. And yes, his fastball was speedier than a racing motorcycle.

Bob Feller went from farm boy to one of the greatest fastball pitchers in baseball.

Catcher Jim Hegan congratulates Bob Feller after Bob pitches the third no-hitter of his career.

BOB "RAPID ROBERT" FELLER

BORN: November 3, 1918

BIRTHPLACE: Van Meter, IA

HEIGHT: 6'0" **WEIGHT:** 185 lbs.

TEAM: Cleveland Indians

BATS: Right

THROWS: Right

POSITION: Pitcher

ROOKIE YEAR: 1936

CAREER ERA: 3.25

THE 25 GREATEST BASEBALL PLAYERS OF ALL TIME

CAREER HIGHLIGHTS: Led the American League in strikeouts from 1938 to 1941 and from 1946 to 1948; led the American League in wins for five consecutive years (with time out for WWII) from 1939 to 1947; voted to eight All-Star Games from 1938 to 1950; pitched a no-hitter in 1940, 1946, and 1951; uniform number (No. 19) was retired in 1957; inducted into the Hall of Fame in 1962

had hit 58 homers that season and was just two away from Babe Ruth's fabled record of 60. The fans saw history that day, but not from Greenberg. Instead they saw the teenage Bob Feller set a new major league record by striking out 18 batters in a game! He led the league in strikeouts that year, with 240, and he would lead the league in strikeouts for the next three years.

The 1940 season started off with a bang. The Indians' first game of the year was in Chicago against the White Sox—and Bob mowed them down, one strikeout after another. The bottom of the ninth arrived, and the White Sox still didn't have a hit. With two outs, Taft Wright hit a hard ground ball to the right side. Second baseman Ray Mack made a tremendous play to get Wright at first. Bob Feller had done it. He had pitched the one and only no-hitter that has ever been thrown on Opening Day. For good measure he pitched two more no-hitters in his career.

The 1940 season didn't end too shabbily either. Bob won the pitching version of the Triple Crown. He led the league in wins, with 27. He had the lowest earned run average (ERA), 2.61. And, of course, he had the most strikeouts: 261.

The following year the Japanese bombed Pearl Harbor in Hawaii, which dragged the United States into World War II. Who was the very first major leaguer to enlist in the military? None other than Bob Feller. It was the prime of his career—he won another 25 games in 1941—but duty called. Bob proceeded to miss three entire baseball seasons while serving his country. He was an antiaircraft gun captain on the USS *Alabama*, and he stayed in shape by running laps around the ship. Bob wasn't just another sailor. By the time he came home, he was highly decorated, with eight battle stars.

Then it was back to baseball. Bob's next full season was 1946. Had he lost anything off his fastball? Quite the contrary. He piled up 26 more wins for the Indians and struck out an incredible 348 batters. That was by far the highest number of strikeouts for any season in his career.

So with all this amazing stuff, have you noticed anything missing? Bob had yet to appear in a World Series. That changed in 1948, when the Indians won the American

Bob Feller is the first major league ball player to enlist in the military after the bombing of Pearl Harbor.

It just may be that Bob had the **FASTEST FASTBALL IN HISTORY**. We'll never know for sure, but once, in Washington, DC, his fastball was clocked at 107.9 miles per hour!

League pennant and squared off against the Boston Braves in the 1948 fall classic. Bob, of course, was chosen to pitch the first game, and he was terrific. He pitched a complete game two-hitter—but Cleveland lost the game 1–0. The Indians then reeled off three straight wins, and Bob was on the mound for Game 5 as the Indians tried to win the World Series at home. His pitching opponent that day was the great lefty, Warren Spahn. Spahn got the better of Bob, and the Braves won the game to stay alive. But the Indians won Game 6, and Bob finally became a world champion.

Bob pitched for another decade, twice more winning 20 games. When he retired in 1956, he had amassed 266 wins and 2,581 strikeouts. He would have easily surpassed 300 wins and 3,000 strikeouts if not for World War II.

As for his honors? He was an eight-time All-Star and had his No. 19 retired by the Indians. There's a Bob Feller museum in his hometown of Van Meter, Iowa. And naturally when he became eligible, he was elected to the Baseball Hall of Fame on the first ballot in 1962.

In describing his pitching style, Bob said, "I just reared back and let them go." Pretty simple. And pretty devastating if you happened to be batting against either "Rapid Robert" or "Bullet Bob" Feller.

Bob Feller winds up for a pitch and shows off his high-kick style.

JOHNNY BENCH

Out of the thousands of players who have donned major league uniforms, we have somehow narrowed down our list to the 25 greatest. What are the odds that some of them would be teammates? The greatest pair of teammates in baseball history would have to be the Yankees' Babe Ruth and Lou Gehrig, but there are several other pairs in this book. In fact, Gehrig was also a teammate of Joe DiMaggio. And DiMaggio was later a teammate of Mickey Mantle. Also in this book, Warren Spahn and Hank Aaron were Braves teammates. But after Ruth and Gehrig, one of the most "dynamic duos" played for Cincinnati's "Big Red Machine"—the all-time hits leader, Pete Rose, and arguably the greatest catcher of all time, Johnny Bench.

Johnny was the complete package of offense and defense. He grew up in the small town of Binger, Oklahoma. Not only did he star on the baseball and basketball teams in high school, but he was also smart. He was the class valedictorian, which meant that he had the highest grades of any graduate. That's kind of funny when you consider that the catcher's equipment is sometimes called "the tools of ignorance."

Johnny was drafted by the Cincinnati Reds when he was only 17 years old. He made it to the majors for part of the 1967 season when he was just 19. He didn't fare too well, hitting just one home run in 26 games. His batting average was a mere .163. Boy, did that change the following year.

It didn't take long for Johnny to establish himself in 1968. He may have officially been a rookie, but he didn't act that way. During a spring-training game, veteran pitcher

Jim Maloney was on the mound. Johnny kept calling for curveballs, but Maloney wanted to throw his fastball. Johnny told him his fastball "wasn't popping." To prove his point, on one fastball, Johnny took off his glove and caught the pitch barehanded. Did that really happen? We're not sure. But it certainly sounds exactly like something Johnny would do. It was around that time that

Johnny met the great Ted Williams. Ted signed an autograph for the young player: "To Johnny Bench, a sure Hall of Famer." Quite a compliment from the greatest hitter of all time.

In 1968 Johnny hit 15 homers, batted .275, and was voted the Rookie of the Year. And he was just getting started. Two years later, he set career highs. He belted 45 homers and drove in 148 runs. That year the Reds won the pennant, and Johnny won the first of his two Most Valuable Player (MVP) Awards.

It wasn't just Johnny's great hitting that earned

JOHNNY BENCH

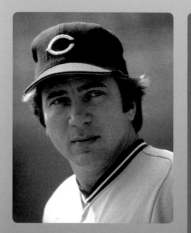

BORN: December 7, 1947

BIRTHPLACE: Oklahoma City, OK

HEIGHT: 6'1" **WEIGHT:** 208 lbs.

TEAM: Cincinnati Reds

BATS: Right

THROWS: Right

POSITION: Catcher

ROOKIE YEAR: 1967

CAREER BATTING AVERAGE: .267

THE 25 GREATEST BASEBALL PLAYERS OF ALL TIME

CAREER HIGHLIGHTS: Voted the National League Rookie of the Year in 1968; won the Rawlings Gold Glove every year from 1968 to 1977; voted to 14 All-Star Games from 1968 to 1983; voted the World Series MVP in 1976; uniform number (No. 5) was retired in 1984; inducted into the Hall of Fame in 1989

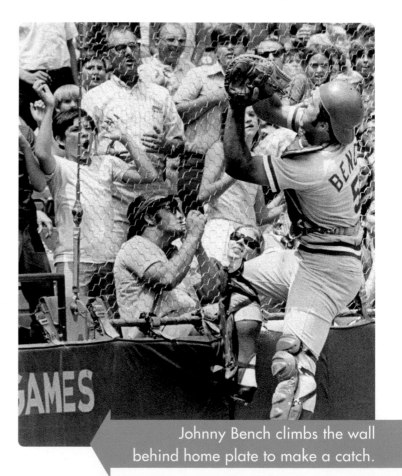

Johnny Bench climbs the wall behind home plate to make a catch.

him his MVP Awards. He was also one of the best defensive catchers who ever played, revolutionizing the position. He was the first catcher to wear a protective helmet behind the plate. And he popularized the one-handed catching style, where he would keep his bare hand behind his body to protect it from foul balls. His great work behind home plate earned him 10 consecutive Gold Glove Awards for fielding.

Led by Johnny and Pete Rose, the Big Red Machine, as the team came to be called, made it to the 1970 and 1972 World Series. The team really had Johnny to thank in 1972. In the fifth and deciding game of the National League Championship Series, the Reds entered the bottom of the ninth inning trailing Pittsburgh 3–2. *Boom!* Johnny promptly hit a home run to tie the game. The Reds then scored the winning run on a wild pitch, and they were off to the World Series. The Reds didn't win in either 1970 or 1972, but they were clearly becoming the "team of the decade."

The Reds made it to two more World Series before the 1970s were over. In 1975 they took on the Boston Red Sox in a classic seven-game series. Johnny hit a home run in Game 3, which Cincinnati won. The Reds won the World Series and Johnny Bench was a world champion. They did it again in 1976.

The 1976 Cincinnati Reds won 102 games, and even

Johnny Bench springs to action to chase a foul ball.

though Johnny was named to the National League All-Star team (he appeared in 14 All-Star Games), he had a sub-par season. That changed big time in the postseason. First the Reds played the Phillies in a best-of-five for the right to get to the World Series. After the Reds won the first two games, they trailed 6–4 going into the bottom of the ninth in Game 3. George Foster and Johnny led off the inning with back-to-back homers. Before the inning was over, the Reds had scored three runs to win the game 7–6 and swept their way into the World Series.

Teammates congratulate Johnny Bench after he hits a home run in the fourth inning of Game 4 in the 1976 World Series.

The 1976 World Series may just have been Johnny Bench's finest hour. The Reds took on the New York Yankees, who had their own great catcher, Thurman Munson. What a battle it was! Munson batted .529 in the 1976 World Series—but Johnny batted an amazing .533!

In the first game, the speedy Mickey Rivers tried to steal second base for the Yankees. Johnny gunned him down. The Yankees never tried to run on Johnny's arm again. In Game 1, Johnny had a triple and double as the Reds won in Cincinnati 5–1. He had two more hits in the second game as the Reds won again. The scene shifted to Yankee Stadium for Game 3, but the result was the same: two more hits for Johnny and another Cincinnati win. The Reds went for the sweep in Game 4, and yup—Johnny got two hits again, only this time they were both home runs. The Reds won the game 7–2 to take back-to-back world championships, and Johnny was named World Series MVP.

The Reds were the first team in the history of the major league playoffs to have a perfect postseason. They went 7–0. It has never happened since, but Johnny's team only had to play one round of playoffs before the World Series, and now there are two.

Johnny played seven more seasons, and as the years went on, he played other positions to take the load off his legs—first, third, and the outfield. He did make it back to the playoffs one more time, in 1979, but the Reds lost to the Pirates. In his last playoff game, he hit his 10th and final postseason home run.

Johnny spent his entire 17-year career with the Reds, and at the time he retired, he held the record for most home runs by a major league catcher. The Reds retired his No. 5, and he was elected to the Baseball Hall of Fame in 1989.

JOHNNY LEE BENCH
CINCINNATI, N.L., 1967-1983
REDEFINED STANDARDS BY WHICH CATCHERS ARE
MEASURED DURING 17 SEASONS WITH "BIG RED MACHINE".
CONTROLLED GAME ON BOTH SIDES OF PLATE WITH
HIS HITTING (389 HOMERS-RECORD 327 AS A CATCHER,
1,376 RBI'S), THROWING OUT OPPOSING BASE RUNNERS,
CALLING PITCHES AND BLOCKING HOME PLATE. N.L.
MVP, 1970 AND 1972. WON 10 GOLD GLOVES. LAST GAME,
9TH INNING HOMER LED TO 1972 PENNANT.

Johnny Bench was elected to the
Hall of Fame in 1989.

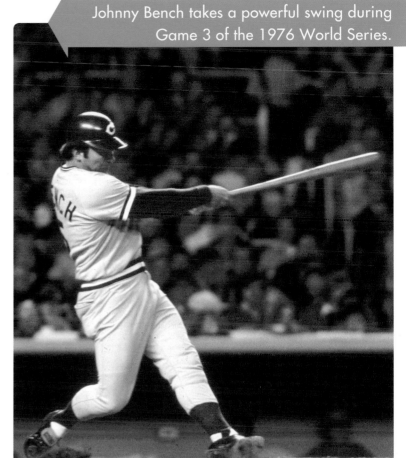

Johnny Bench takes a powerful swing during
Game 3 of the 1976 World Series.

The distance
from home plate to
second base is 127 feet.

Johnny Bench's father taught him to throw twice
that distance, 254 feet, from a crouching position!
It's no wonder that Johnny boasted, **"I CAN
THROW OUT ANY RUNNER ALIVE."**

And how's this for another honor? The best college
baseball catcher every year is awarded the Johnny Bench
Award. It's just one more indication that when it comes
to all the people who put on the "tools of ignorance,"
nobody did it better than Johnny Bench.

JIMMIE
FOXX

ere's something that Hall of Fame pitcher Lefty Gomez once said: "When Neil Armstrong first set foot on the moon in 1969, he and all the space scientists were puzzled by an unidentifiable white object. I knew immediately what it was. That was a home run ball hit off me in 1933 by Jimmie Foxx."

When it came to home-run sluggers back in the day, first came Babe Ruth. Then from the right side of the plate came Jimmie Foxx.

Jimmie grew up in rural Sudlersville, Maryland. Like so many other athletes, he built up his strength working on a farm. He stood 6 feet tall and weighed 195 pounds, but people thought he was so much bigger because he hit the ball so far. One of his nicknames was "the Beast."

Jimmie started out as a catcher and made it to the Philadelphia A's in 1925 when he was just 17. When Jimmie arrived on the scene, the A's already had a future Hall of Famer at catcher—Mickey Cochrane—so Jimmie didn't play that much. He only batted nine times in 1925, but he had six hits. And so it went for the next three years. Jimmie didn't have a full-time position, but he batted over .300 each season.

By 1929 the A's manager, Connie Mack, knew he had to find a position for this terrific hitter, so Jimmie became a first baseman. And what a season he had! He belted 33 homers, thus beginning a record streak where he hit 30 or more homers for 12 straight years. He also knocked in 118 runs and batted .354 in 1929.

Led by the Beast, the A's made it to their first World Series in 15 years, taking on the Chicago Cubs. The first game was scoreless until the seventh inning, when Jimmie hit a homer. The A's went on to win the game 3–1. Game 2 was scoreless in the third inning. With two outs, Jimmie came to the plate with two men on. You guessed it—a three-run homer! The A's were on their way to winning the World Series in five games.

The next year they did it again. In 1930 Jimmie increased his home-run total to 37 and drove in an amazing 156 runs. The A's easily won the American League pennant and faced the St. Louis Cardinals in the World Series. Game 5 was pivotal. The Series was tied at two games apiece, and the game in St. Louis was scoreless in the top of the ninth. With one out, Mickey Cochrane walked. Next up to the plate was Jimmie. He was facing a future Hall of Fame pitcher named Burleigh Grimes.

The spitball was outlawed in baseball in 1920, but all the pitchers who were throwing it at the time were permitted to continue "loading up" the baseball. Grimes was the last remaining legal spitball pitcher when he faced Jimmie in the 1930 World Series. Dry or wet, it didn't matter. Jimmie hit a game-winning two-run homer. Two days later the A's won another World Series, and again it had been Jimmie with the big blasts. The following year they lost the World Series to the Cardinals, but in his three World Series, Jimmie hit .344 with four home runs. Talk about rising to the occasion!

A big reason why the A's didn't win another pennant after that was money. Connie Mack, the manager, was

500 HOME RUNS CLUB
Total Home Runs
534

Jimmie Foxx reaches for a ball during a pregame warm up.

also an owner of the A's, and when attendance faltered, he broke up the team to save money. But Mack kept Jimmie on board, and he proceeded to have some unforgettable seasons. Jimmy nearly won the Triple Crown in 1932, leading the league with 58 homers and 169 runs batted in (RBIs). He would have tied Babe Ruth's record of 60 homers, but two home runs that he hit didn't count, because the games got rained out before they became official. He won his first Most Valuable Player (MVP) Award that season.

The next year Jimmie did win the Triple Crown, and another MVP Award. He continued to pile up incredible numbers. But after the 1935 season, and despite all he had done, he was asked to take a pay cut. He refused, and Mack traded him to the Boston Red Sox for a couple of players and $150,000.

Jimmie Foxx was so feared as a hitter that he was walked over 100 times in six different seasons.

At the age of 28, Jimmie was far from finished. For the next five seasons, he continued to belt homers and drive in runs at a dizzying pace. In 1938 he again hit 50 homers, and he drove in an unbelievable 175 runs, earning him his third MVP Award. One game from that year really stands out. On June 16, the Red Sox played the Browns in St. Louis. The box score read 0–0–0 next to Jimmie's name for times at bat, hits, and RBIs. But Jimmie came to the plate six times that day and walked every time. (A walk doesn't count as an at-bat in-the-box score.) That's an American League record that still stands today.

By the time he finished playing in 1945, Jimmie had eclipsed the 500 home-run mark. He was the second man and the first righty hitter to do it. His 534 homers, at the time, were second only to Babe Ruth. It was another two decades before Willie Mays came along to beat out Foxx for second place.

All these years later, Jimmie still ranks in the top 20.

Jimmie Foxx was elected to the Baseball Hall of Fame in 1951, but even though he wore No. 3 (the same number as the Babe) with both the A's and Red Sox, he never had his number retired by either club.

AMERICAN LEAGUE
TRIPLE CROWN WINNER

1933
48 HR, 163 RBIs, .356 BA

JIMMIE "THE BEAST" FOXX

BORN: October 22, 1907
BIRTHPLACE: Sudlersville, MD
HEIGHT: 6'0" **WEIGHT:** 195 lbs.
TEAMS: Philadelphia Athletics, Boston Red Sox
BATS: Right **THROWS:** Right
POSITION: First baseman
ROOKIE YEAR: 1925
CAREER BATTING AVERAGE: .325

THE **25** GREATEST BASEBALL PLAYERS OF ALL TIME

CAREER HIGHLIGHTS: Voted the American League MVP in 1932, 1933, and 1938; led the American League in batting average in 1932, 1933, and 1938; led the American League in home runs in 1932, 1933, 1935, and 1939; won the American League Triple Crown for batting in 1933; voted to every All-Star Game from 1933 to 1941; inducted into the Hall of Fame in 1951

When the A's were in Philadelphia, they were managed by legendary Hall of Famer **CONNIE MACK**. He managed the team for half a century— from 1901 to 1950! During that time they won **NINE PENNANTS AND FIVE WORLD SERIES.**

BOB GIBSON

According to my Blue Ribbon Panel, the 25 players in this book arc the greatest who ever played the game. It turns out that I've met over half of them—13, to be exact. And there's one I co-hosted a TV show with: Bob Gibson. In 1979 we hosted a baseball program on HBO called *Race for the Pennant*. That TV show is long forgotten, but Bob's brilliant baseball career will be remembered forever. Here's the story of how a poor, sickly kid from Omaha, Nebraska, who was first a basketball star became one of the most feared pitchers to ever toe the rubber.

When Bob was a kid growing up in Omaha, nobody could have predicted his success. Heck, doctors didn't think he'd still be alive to even have a career in baseball. Bob was born to a very poor family in 1935. He had any number of ailments, including rickets, asthma, and a heart murmur, and if that wasn't enough, he nearly died of pneumonia. And yet he overcame all of that to become a terrific young athlete.

In high school, Bob was excellent at track and basketball in addition to baseball. How great was he at basketball? He received a scholarship to play hoops for Creighton University. While he was at Creighton, he also starred on the baseball team. And that was where he caught the attention of the St. Louis Cardinals. In 1957 the Cards paid Bob all of $4,000 to sign a contract, but he delayed his baseball career and spent a year playing basketball for the famed Harlem Globetrotters.

When Bob finally turned his attention to baseball, he spent a couple of years in the minors before he finally made it to the major leagues—and he wasn't an immediate success. Sure, he could throw the ball hard, but not always where he wanted it. In fact, the only category in which he led the National League was bases on balls! In short, his first three seasons in the big leagues gave little indication of what was to come.

BOB GIBSON

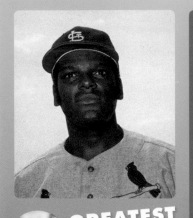

GREATEST
25 BASEBALL PLAYERS
OF ALL TIME

BORN: November 9, 1935

BIRTHPLACE: Omaha, NE

HEIGHT: 6'2" **WEIGHT:** 195 lbs.

TEAM: St. Louis Cardinals

BATS: Right

THROWS: Right

POSITION: Pitcher

ROOKIE YEAR: 1959

CAREER ERA: 2.91

CAREER HIGHLIGHTS: Voted to eight All-Star Games from 1962 to 1972; voted the World Series MVP in 1964 and 1967; won the Rawlings Gold Glove every year from 1965 to 1973; voted the National League MVP in 1968; won the National League Cy Young Award in 1968 and 1970; pitched a no-hitter in 1971; inducted into the Hall of Fame in 1981

Tim McCarver, who went on to have a fabulous career as a sportscaster, was Bob's catcher in St. Louis. One time when McCarver went to the mound to settle Bob down, Bob scowled at him and barked that "the only thing you know about pitching is how hard it is to hit." That's the way Bob was on the mound: fiercely competitive.

Then came 1964, a magical year in Cardinals history and Bob was the chief magician. The Cardinals were involved in a tight pennant race among three teams: the Cards, the Reds, and the fading Phillies. While fighting for the pennant, Bob went to the mound 11 times and registered 9 wins! It all came down to the final game of the season. Bob pitched in relief and beat the Mets. The Cards were National League champs by one slim game over both Philadelphia and Cincinnati. They went to the World Series against the powerful Yankees.

Bob was tagged with the loss in Game 2, but he came back strong in Game 5. He struck out 13 and pitched a ten-inning complete game for the win. Game 7 was even more remarkable. Bob pitched on just two days' rest, but he beat the Yankees again, and the Cards won their first

Bob started to turn the corner in 1962, when he improved his control. Then in 1963 he had his breakthrough season: he went 18–9. But the best was yet to come. Over the next decade, he was a perennial All-Star, as well as a Gold Glove winner for fielding. And he pitched "mean." He was an intimidating pitcher. If a batter dared to crowd the plate, a fastball would come zinging inside.

3,000 STRIKEOUTS CLUB
Total Strikeouts
3,117

championship in 18 years. Bob was named World Series Most Valuable Player (MVP).

What happened three years later in the 1967 World Series was even more remarkable—and it almost never happened at all. In July, the great Roberto Clemente of the Pirates had rocketed a line drive that broke Bob's leg. It took him nearly two months to return. And when he did, he won his first three games, the third one clinching the National League pennant for St. Louis.

The 1967 World Series featured the Cardinals against the Boston Red Sox. The Red Sox were led by Triple Crown winner Carl Yastrzemski, and they were dubbed "the Impossible Dream." Bob became their impossible nightmare. He pitched a complete-game victory in Game 1. Then in Game 4, he pitched a complete-game shutout. And for his grand finale, pitching on three

The **"STRETCH RUN"** is the end of the season when teams are battling to make the postseason. It refers to the season coming down the home stretch.

Teammates congratulate Bob Gibson after he pitches a complete game and wins against the Boston Red Sox during the 1967 World Series.

Bob Gibson pitched a no-hitter on August 14, 1971, against Pittsburgh. The final score was 11–0.

in the World Series. But even though he again pitched three complete games, he lost Game 7.

By the time Bob retired in 1975, he was the winningest pitcher in Cards history and just the second pitcher after Walter Johnson to eclipse 3,000 strikeouts. He was a two-time Cy Young Award winner, an eight-time All-Star, and a nine-time Gold Glove winner. Did I mention

days' rest, he not only pitched a complete game to win Game 7 at Fenway Park, he also hit a homer! He is one of only six pitchers in baseball history to pitch three complete-game victories in a single World Series. Of course, he was named Series MVP.

Bob nearly duplicated that feat the next year, 1968, which may have been the single most incredible season that a pitcher has ever had. To say that Bob was dominant doesn't even begin to tell the story. Here are a few numbers: During a 92-inning stretch, he allowed just two earned runs. He threw 13 shutouts, which led the National League, as did his 268 strikeouts. He also pitched 28 complete games.

Think about that—13 shutouts and 28 complete games in one season. Most pitchers today don't total those numbers for an entire career! But here's the real stunner. His earned run average (ERA) for the entire 1968 season was a puny 1.12. That's a record that still stands today. His win-loss record was 22–9, and that doesn't count two more wins in the World Series against the Tigers. Bob not only won the Cy Young Award as the best pitcher in the league, he was also named the MVP. After that incredible regular season, he beat the Detroit Tigers twice

Bob Gibson proudly holds his Gold Glove Award.

that he also pitched a no-hitter in 1971 against Pittsburgh?

Here are a couple more records. Bob recorded 35 strikeouts in the 1968 World Series, and 17 in one game—records that still stand. His No. 45 was retired by the Cardinals, and in 1981 he was elected to the Baseball Hall of Fame.

A short conversation between two ballplayers helps to sum up the competitive spirit of Bob. Dusty Baker had a modest 17-game hitting streak when he was playing for the Atlanta Braves. His teammate, the great Hank Aaron, gave him some advice about hitting against Bob. Hank said, "Don't dig in against Bob Gibson; he'll knock you down. Don't stare at him. He doesn't like it. If you happen to hit a home run, don't run too slow, don't run too fast. If you want to celebrate, get in the tunnel first. And if he hits you, don't charge the mound, because he's a Gold Glove boxer."

Needless to say, Dusty Baker's hitting streak ended that night. But he certainly wasn't the only one who had trouble hitting against perhaps the most feared righty pitcher of all time, Bob Gibson.

Bob Gibson pitches against the Detroit Tigers during the 1968 World Series.

After Bob Gibson's spectacular 1968 season, Major League Baseball changed some rules. For example, the height of the pitcher's mound was lowered to help hitters. Did lowering the mound affect Bob? Not really. He won 20 games in 1969 and a career-high 23 in 1970.

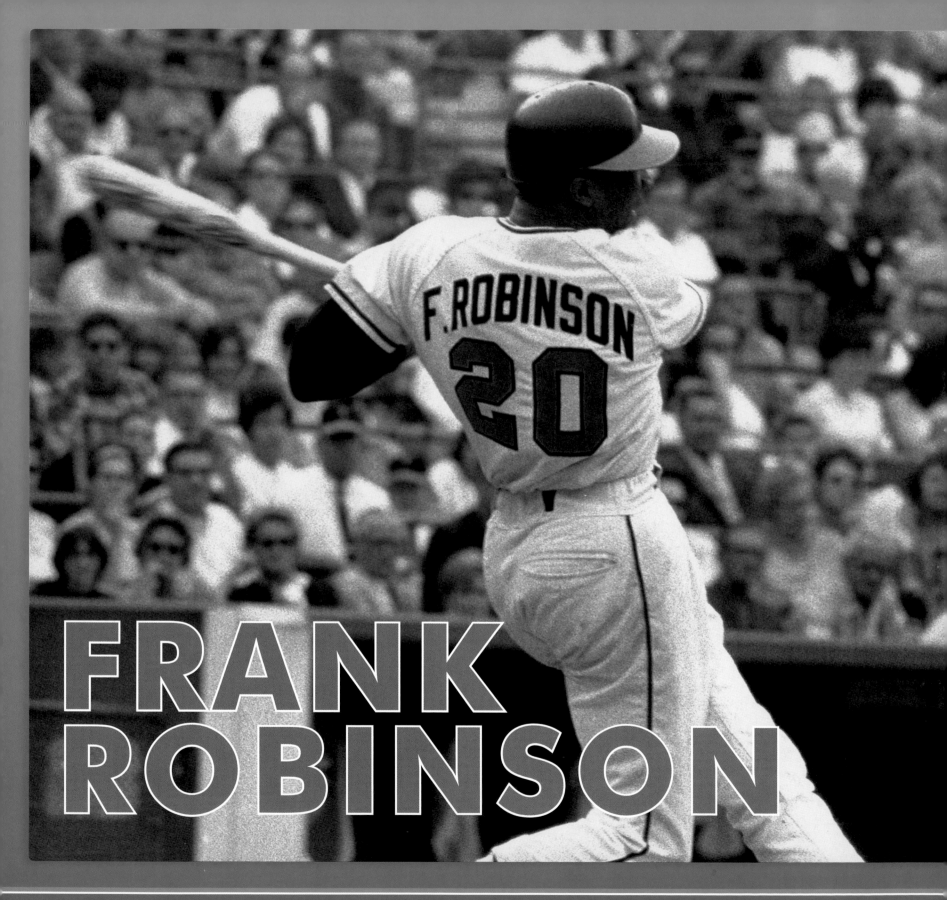

FRANK ROBINSON

The worst baseball deal of all time had to be when the Boston Red Sox sold Babe Ruth to the New York Yankees for $100,000 in 1919. The second-worst deal? That may have been in 1965, when the Cincinnati Reds traded their "old" outfielder, Frank Robinson, to the Baltimore Orioles. Frank was all of 30 years old, and the next year in Baltimore, he proceeded to have one of the greatest seasons in the history of baseball.

Frank grew up in Oakland, California, and attended McClymonds High School. He played basketball on the same team as NBA Hall of Famer Bill Russell. What a basketball team that must have been, featuring future Hall of Famers from two different sports!

In 1953 the Cincinnati Reds signed Frank to a contract with a $3,500 bonus. And three years later he made it to the major leagues. What a rookie year! He tied the record, at the time, for most home runs by a rookie, with 38, and he led the entire National League in runs scored, with 122. That year he was voted to start in left field in the 1956 All-Star Game, where he was a star among stars. No less than seven of the players who played in that game are featured in this book. The National League won the game 7–3 with Hall of Famers Willie Mays, Stan Musial, Ted Williams, and Mickey Mantle all hitting home runs. Frank's first major league season was capped off by winning the National League Rookie of the Year Award.

Frank was not only a great hitter, he was fearless. He would crowd home plate, daring opposing pitchers to hit him. And hit him they did. He was hit by a pitch 20 times in his rookie year, the highest number for any player in the league. Managers would tell their players not to throw at Frank, because it only made him angry and more aggressive at the plate. Frank would say that after he was thrown at, he would get up, dust himself off, and be more determined than ever to get a hit.

Frank Robinson is the **CHAMP OF "DOUBLING UP"** on records. Not only was he the first to win the MVP in both leagues, he was the first to hit 200 homers in both leagues; he was the first to hit All-Star homers for both leagues; and he was the first black manager in both leagues. (He was named manager of the San Francisco Giants in 1981.)

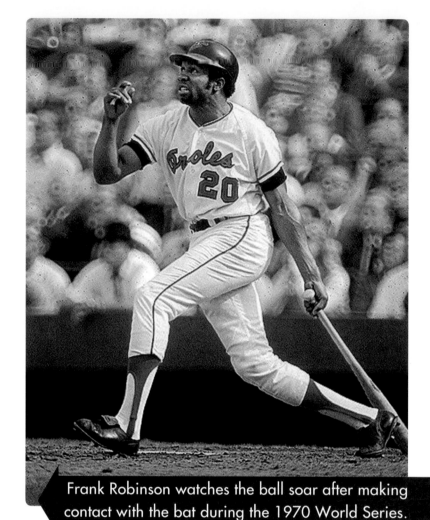

Frank Robinson watches the ball soar after making contact with the bat during the 1970 World Series.

Over the next several seasons, Frank continued to pile up impressive numbers. Then in 1961 he belted 37 homers and drove in 124 runs while batting .323. It earned him the first of his two Most Valuable Player (MVP) Awards. Even more importantly, he led the Reds to their first National League pennant since 1940. Cincinnati then faced the powerful Yankees in the World Series. The Yanks were led by Mickey Mantle and Roger Maris—that season Maris had broken Babe Ruth's record by hitting 61 home runs. Unfortunately for the Reds, the Yankees easily won the World Series in five games.

Frank was even greater the following year. He hit more homers (39), drove in more runs (136), and had a higher batting average (.342) than he did in 1961. On top of that, he led the league with 134 runs scored. But the Reds finished in third place and never got back to the World Series with Frank on their team. In 1965, despite another

All-Star Game appearance for Frank, the owner of the Reds decided that he was "an old 30" and traded him to Baltimore for three players. It turned out to be one of the most lopsided trades in the history of baseball.

Frank turned an even "older" 31 during the 1966 season, and boy, did he accomplish a lot that year. He led the American League with a career-high 49 homers. He also drove in 122 runs and scored 122, leading the league in both categories. And his .316 batting average led the league, as well. In short, he won the Triple Crown! Not bad for an "old" guy. On May 8, he crushed a fastball thrown by Luis Tiant of Cleveland for a homer. It was the only fair ball ever hit clear out of Memorial Stadium in Baltimore. Of course, he won the 1966 American League MVP Award, thus becoming the only player in baseball history to win the MVP in both leagues.

But there's more. Led by Frank's amazing season, the Orioles ran away with the American League pennant and faced the Los Angeles Dodgers in the World Series. In Game 1 against the great fastball pitcher Don Drysdale, Frank drilled a long home run his first time up. He had two hits and two runs batted in (RBIs) as the Orioles won the game 5–2.

After winning Games 2 and 3, the Orioles went for the sweep in Baltimore, once again facing Don Drysdale. In the fourth inning, Frank hit another home run. It was the only run of the game, as the Orioles swept the Dodgers to win their first-ever world championship. Frank was voted the World Series MVP.

This was far from the last World Series

500 HOME RUNS CLUB
Total Home Runs
556

appearance Frank's Orioles would make. They went to the fall classic three straight years—1969, 1970, and 1971. In 1969 they were upset by the "Miracle Mets," and

FRANK ROBINSON

THE **25** GREATEST BASEBALL PLAYERS OF ALL TIME

BORN: August 31, 1935
BIRTHPLACE: Beaumont, TX
HEIGHT: 6'1" **WEIGHT:** 195 lbs.
TEAMS: Cincinnati Reds, Baltimore Orioles, Los Angeles Dodgers, California Angels, Cleveland Indians
BATS: Right
THROWS: Right
POSITION: Designated hitter
ROOKIE YEAR: 1956
BATTING AVERAGE: .294

CAREER HIGHLIGHTS: Voted the National League Rookie of the Year in 1956; won the Rawlings Gold Glove in 1958; voted to 14 All-Star Games from 1957 to 1974; voted the National League MVP in 1961 and the American League MVP in 1966; won the American League Triple Crown for batting in 1966; voted the World Series MVP in 1966; voted the All-Star MVP in 1971; uniform number (No. 20) was retired by Baltimore in 1972 and by Cincinnati in 1998; inducted into the Hall of Fame in 1982

then in 1970 Frank got to face his old team, the Cincinnati Reds, in the World Series. Revenge was sweet. Frank hit two homers as the Orioles beat the Reds in five games.

In the 1971 World Series, the Orioles lost to the Pittsburgh Pirates in seven games, despite two more homers from Frank. All in all, Frank appeared in 26 World Series games, hitting eight homers while driving in 14 runs. Not bad on the biggest stage in baseball. For his career Frank hit 586 homers, and when he retired from playing in 1976, only Hank Aaron, Babe Ruth, and Willie Mays had hit more home runs. But none of them did what Frank did on June 26, 1970, against Washington. In the fifth inning, he hit a grand slam, and then his next time up, the very next inning, he hit another grand slam!

There was more history for Frank to make. In 1975 he was named player/manager of the Cleveland Indians. It was groundbreaking. Frank had become the first black manager in the history of Major League Baseball. And how's this for a debut? On Opening Day he penciled his own name into the lineup as the designated hitter against the New York Yankees. His first time up, he hit a homer, and the Indians beat the Yankees 5–3 in his managerial debut. It was the eighth home run that Frank hit on an Opening Day. That record has since been tied by Ken Griffey Jr. Frank went on to manage three more teams, and with Baltimore in 1989, he was voted Manager of the Year. What a collection of awards!

Player/manager Frank Robinson submits his batting lineup to an umpire before a game. Frank was the first African American manager in Major League history.

Hank Aaron (L) and Frank Robinson pose together after being voted into the Major League Baseball Hall of Fame.

Here are some more honors. His No. 20 was retired by two teams, Baltimore and Cincinnati. There's a bronze statue of Frank outside the Great American Ball Park in Cincinnati. And in 2005 Frank was awarded the Presidential Medal of Freedom by President George W. Bush.

Frank was elected to the Baseball Hall of Fame in 1982. During his acceptance speech that day in Cooperstown, he told the crowd, "I don't see anyone playing in the major leagues today who combines both the talent and the intensity that I had. I always tried to do the best. I knew I couldn't always be the best, but I tried to be."

What confidence. And what great words to live by.

Frank Robinson was the league leader in the category of "hit by pitch" seven different times. By the end of his career, **HE WAS HIT AN ASTOUNDING 198 TIMES!**

CHRISTY MATHEWSON

New York City has had more than its share of baseball heroes. Just look at this book and you'll see some of the greatest to play in the Big Apple: Babe Ruth, Lou Gehrig, Joe DiMaggio, Mickey Mantle, Alex Rodriguez, and Willie Mays. But who was the first New York baseball hero? None of the above. He didn't even play for the Yankees. He is Christy Mathewson, and he pitched for the New York Giants. In fact, he was one of the United States' first sports heroes of any kind.

Let me tell you about the 1905 World Series. Christy's Giants were playing the Philadelphia A's in the second-ever World Series. Christy pitched the first game in Philadelphia and threw a complete-game, four-hit shutout as the Giants won 3–0. These days, the standard rest for a pitcher between starts is four days. But pitching on just two days' rest, Christy took the mound for Game 3, and guess what? He pitched another four-hit shutout. This time the final score was 9–0.

For Game 5 at the Polo Grounds in New York, Christy took the mound again—this time after just one day of rest! But he didn't pitch a four-hitter in this game. He pitched a complete-game, five-hit shutout. Christy pitched three shutouts in six days as the Giants won the World Series four games to one. But I'm getting ahead of myself. I just wanted to give you a quick idea of what an incredible pitcher Christy Mathewson was.

Christy was born in 1880 in a town called Factoryville, Pennsylvania, near Scranton. Like most players of his era, he grew up on a farm. But unlike most baseball players, he went to college. Christy attended Bucknell University, where he not only played baseball and football, he was also the class president and sang in the glee club. You'd have to say he was pretty well-rounded.

CHRISTY MATHEWSON

THE 25 GREATEST BASEBALL PLAYERS OF ALL TIME

BORN: August 12, 1880

BIRTHPLACE: Factoryville, PA

HEIGHT: 6'2" **WEIGHT:** 195 lbs.

TEAM: New York Giants

BATS: Right

THROWS: Right

POSITION: Pitcher

ROOKIE YEAR: 1900

CAREER ERA: 2.13

CAREER HIGHLIGHTS: Won the National League Triple Crown for pitching in 1905 and 1908; pitched no-hitters in 1901 and 1905; tied for third-most wins in a career (373); uniform was retired in 1988; inducted into the Hall of Fame in 1936

Christy Mathewson was a very economical pitcher. He **RARELY WALKED A BATTER**, and it wouldn't be unusual for him to pitch a complete game by throwing just 75 or 80 pitches. Nowadays, when a pitcher reaches 100 pitches around the sixth or seventh inning, he's taken out of the game.

After college he signed with the New York Giants for $1,500. In 1900 he was so bad in his first three games that the Giants sent him back to the minor leagues and demanded their money back. But the next year, he was back with the Giants, and his career took off. He won 20 games in 1901, including a no-hitter against the Cardinals. After dipping to just 14 wins the following year, he never won fewer than 22 games every season until 1914.

Now let's go back to that amazing 1905 World Series when he pitched those three shutouts. His regular season was just as incredible. Now granted, he was pitching in the so-called "dead-ball era," when there weren't a lot of home runs, but Christy was simply the best of the best. That year he won 31 games, and eight of them were shutouts. He struck out 106 batters, and his earned run average (ERA) was a microscopic 1.28. He led the National League in every one of those categories. He even pitched his second career no-hitter that year against the Cubs. There was no Cy Young Award back then—heck, Young was still pitching for the Boston Red Sox in 1905—but if there had been such an award, Christy would have won it hands down.

You've probably heard of a pitch called the "screwball." Christy was the pitcher who made it famous. At the time it was known as a "fadeaway." When a righty pitcher

All sorts of pitches have been used by ballplayers to strike out their opponents throughout the years. Some of these pitches have great names like the screwball, spitball (outlawed in 1920), slider, knuckleball, sinker, splitter, and dry spitter.

Christy Mathewson poses for a photo during practice.

NATIONAL LEAGUE
TRIPLE CROWN WINNER

1905
31 wins, 1.28 ERA, 206 strikeouts

1908
37 wins, 1.43 ERA, 259 strikeouts

to have an overpowering fastball, and he wasn't very intimidating on the mound, but his variety of pitches and his pinpoint control combined to make him one of the greatest pitchers who ever played.

Christy's only championship was in 1905, but his 1908 season was simply phenomenal. He won 37 games, and 34 of those wins were complete games, with 11 shutouts. And yes, he also led the league in strikeouts, ERA, and just about every other pitching category. By comparison, if you fast-forward 100 years to 2008, the best pitcher in the National League was also a Giant—a San Francisco Giant—Tim Lincecum. He won the Cy Young Award. But where Christy won 37 games, Lincecum won just 18, and he only pitched two complete games and just one shutout. How times have changed for pitchers with the heavy use of the bullpen by major league managers!

throws a curve, the pitch will break away from a righty hitter. That's the reason why managers like to put lefty hitters up to bat against righty pitchers—a curveball will break closer to the batter. Well, the screwball is just the opposite. It curves in toward a righty hitter, and away from a lefty. When Christy started throwing the screwball, it was considered a new pitch. He wasn't known

Christy led the New York Giants to three more World Series in 1911, 1912, and 1913. The 1911 World Series started out like the 1905 World Series for Christy. He won the first game against the Philadelphia A's, and he started Game 3 on just two days' rest. He pitched eleven innings that day but lost the game 3–2. The Giants wound up losing

CHRISTY MATHEWSON'S LEADING CAREER STATS

CATEGORY	RANK
Wins	#3 (373—tied with G. Alexander)
Shutouts	#3 (79)
ERA	#6 (2.13)

that World Series and the next two, as well. Christy pitched another complete-game shutout in Game 2 of the 1913 World Series, but it was the only game the Giants won in the Series that year. Christy never made it back to another World Series.

All in all Christy pitched for 17 seasons, and when he retired, he had amassed 373 career wins. That's good for third place on the all-time list behind two other pitchers in this book, Cy Young and Walter Johnson. Christy's 79 shutouts also rank third. He even had more shutouts than the great Cy Young.

When it came time to open the Baseball Hall of Fame in Cooperstown, there were only five players voted to

Christy Mathewson was a very religious man, and he **NEVER PITCHED ON SUNDAY**. That wasn't a big problem back then, because some of the cities in the league wouldn't allow baseball games to be played on Sundays.

The 1912 New York Giants. Christy Mathewson is in the front row, fifth from the right.

the first class in 1936: Babe Ruth, Ty Cobb, Walter Johnson, Honus Wagner, and Christy Mathewson. Christy had enlisted in the Army to fight in World War I, and in a terrible training accident, he was exposed to poison gas. As a result he developed tuberculosis and died at the age of just 45. So at Cooperstown he was inducted into the Hall of Fame posthumously, which means he was inducted after he had passed away.

In addition to making the Hall of Fame, Christy is also remembered in his hometown of Factoryville, Pennsylvania. Every August to this day, the townspeople hold Christy Mathewson Day. They have a parade, a running race, a lot of food, and other fun activities.

Christy may have stopped playing baseball 100 years ago, but he is still celebrated as one of the greatest pitchers in the history of the game. And his love of baseball is summed up by something he once said: "A boy cannot begin playing ball too early. I might almost say that while he is still creeping on all fours he should have a bouncing rubber ball."

The way he pitched, Christy must have started even earlier than that!

300 WINS CLUB
Total Wins
373

CHRISTY MATHEWSON
NEW YORK, N.L., 1900-1916.
CINCINNATI, N.L., 1916.
BORN FACTORYVILLE, PA., AUGUST 12, 1880
GREATEST OF ALL THE GREAT PITCHERS
IN THE 20TH CENTURY'S FIRST QUARTER
PITCHED 3 SHUTOUTS IN 1905 WORLD SERIES.
FIRST PITCHER OF THE CENTURY EVER TO
WIN 30 GAMES IN 3 SUCCESSIVE YEARS.
WON 37 GAMES IN 1908
"MATTY WAS MASTER OF THEM ALL"

Christy Mathewson was elected to the Hall of Fame in 1936.

Christy Mathewson was the most famous athlete to ever play at Bucknell. The school's football stadium today is named **CHRISTY MATHEWSON-MEMORIAL STADIUM.**

JACKIE ROBINSON

The baseball players in this book are all great, no question about it. But who is the most *significant* baseball player of all time? You can make a case for Babe Ruth, but I think one name tops them all—not just in terms of baseball, but for all of professional sports: Jackie Robinson.

Jackie was born in the small town of Cairo, Georgia, in 1919. He was the youngest of five kids and was raised by a single mother. His family was poor, and they loved sports. Jackie's older brother, Mack, helped to inspire him. At the 1936 Berlin Olympics, Mack won the silver medal in the 200-meter dash, right behind gold medalist and sports legend Jesse Owens.

As for Jackie, he not only loved sports, he was great at all of them. In high school, and then in college at UCLA, he starred in baseball, basketball, football, and track. In fact, he was the first athlete in UCLA history to earn varsity letters in four sports. So in addition to being one of the greatest baseball players of all time, Jackie was one of the greatest all-around American athletes.

Jackie first entered pro sports as a football player. He was 22 years old in 1941 when he moved to Honolulu, Hawaii. He joined the Honolulu Bears, a semipro team, but his football career was cut short by the bombing of Pearl Harbor. Like many young Americans, Jackie entered the military, but he never fought in World War II. Those were the days of segregation. If a black person got on a bus, he or she had to sit in the back. One day Jackie refused to go to the back of the bus, and he was put on trial. He was found innocent, but because of the trial, he wasn't sent overseas to fight.

At the time, Major League Baseball was also segregated. The first half-century of baseball has wonderful stories about great players like Babe Ruth, Cy Young, and Ty Cobb. Those great players had one thing in common: they never played against black players in the major leagues. African American players were forced to play in the Negro Leagues. So after the war, Jackie joined up with the Negro League team in Kansas City, the Monarchs. He immediately became a sensation—so much so that Brooklyn Dodgers president Branch Rickey decided that

"I'm not concerned with your liking or disliking me...All I ask is that you respect me as a human being."

—JACKIE ROBINSON

Jackie was worthy of becoming the first black player to play in the majors.

Rickey knew that "breaking the color barrier" would be incredibly hard for Jackie. So he gave Jackie an important piece of advice that he carried with him the rest of his life: Don't get angry, and don't fight back. Concentrate on baseball.

Jackie joined the minor league Montreal Royals, a Brooklyn Dodgers farm team, in the spring of 1946. In his very first game, Jackie batted 4 for 5 against

Jersey City—including a three-run homer, four runs batted in (RBIs), and two stolen bases. And he never let up. Bigoted fans would yell nasty things at him from the stands. He even received death threats. But Jackie took Branch Rickey's advice to heart and didn't respond. He let his baseball do his talking for him.

Jackie Robinson's teammates congratulate him after he hits a two-run homer in a game against Pittsburgh.

That year he led the Royals to the "Little World Series" championship.

He was ready for the major leagues. It was now time to make history.

The date was April 15, 1947. The place: Ebbets Field, Brooklyn. Jackie became the first black man to play in a Major League Baseball game. He didn't get a hit that day, but he had a key bunt in the seventh inning, and he wound up scoring the winning run as the Brooklyn Dodgers beat the Boston Braves 5–3. The baseball part was easy for Jackie. The rest was very tough to deal with. He was taunted by fans, as well as by opposing players and managers. Even some of Jackie's own teammates threatened to strike if they were forced to play with him. But Dodgers manager Leo Durocher remained loyal, telling everyone on the team that he'd trade all of them before Jackie.

That first season Jackie was voted the National League Rookie of the Year. He batted .297 with 12 home runs and 29 stolen bases, helping the Dodgers win the National League pennant. Two years later he won the National League Most Valuable Player (MVP) Award. In 1949 he led the league in hitting and stolen bases—a .342 batting average to go with 37 steals. And he again helped the Dodgers win the pennant. But those early years were incredibly difficult for Jackie.

JACKIE ROBINSON

THE 25 GREATEST BASEBALL PLAYERS OF ALL TIME

BORN: January 31, 1919

BIRTHPLACE: Cairo, GA

HEIGHT: 5'11" **WEIGHT:** 204 lbs.

TEAM: Brooklyn Dodgers

BATS: Right

THROWS: Right

POSITION: Second Baseman

ROOKIE YEAR: 1947

CAREER BATTING AVERAGE: .311

CAREER HIGHLIGHTS: First African American baseball player in the major leagues; voted the National League Rookie of the Year in 1947; led the National League in stolen bases in 1947 and 1949; voted to every All-Star Game from 1949 to 1954; voted the National League MVP in 1949; led the National League in batting average in 1949 (.342); inducted into the Hall of Fame in 1962; uniform number (No. 42) was retired by every team in the major leagues in 1997

There was one game in Cincinnati that really stood out. The fans were screaming and heckling Jackie. Finally Dodgers shortstop Pee Wee Reese walked over and put his arm around Jackie. That silenced the crowd. Jackie said it was a moment that he would never forget.

During Game 1 of the 1955 World Series, Jackie Robinson successfully steals home.

Jackie's crowning baseball moment came in 1955, when the Dodgers played the New York Yankees in the World Series. Jackie and the Dodgers had been in four World Series, and they had lost to the Yankees all four times. In Game 1 of the 1955 World Series, the Dodgers were trailing 6–4 in the eighth inning. Then came one of the most exciting plays in World Series history. Jackie danced off third base with the great Yankee pitcher Whitey Ford on the mound, and then

he took off for home. He slid in safe! Jackie had stolen home, one of the rarest plays you'll ever see, and he did it in the World Series. The Dodgers wound up winning a thrilling seven-game series. Jackie and the Brooklyn Dodgers were finally World Series champions.

Jackie played 10 years in the majors and finished with a career .311 batting average. He was selected to the All-Star Game six times, and needless to say, Jackie was inducted into the Baseball Hall of Fame in the first year he was eligible. During his induction speech in 1962, he gracefully alluded to the tough times he had to endure. "I want to thank all of the people throughout this country who were so wonderful during those trying days."

In 1997, Jackie Robinson's No. 42 was the very first (and only) number to be retired across all teams in the Major Leagues.

Jackie Robinson was inducted into the Baseball Hall of Fame on July 23, 1962.

At the beginning of Major League games, there is a tradition known as the "ceremonial first pitch." This is a pitch thrown before the game begins by someone of particular significance. Over the years everyone from presidents to musicians to actors to military veterans has had the chance to throw the very first pitch of the game!

Fifty years to the day after Jackie broke baseball's color barrier, on April 15, 1997, a ceremony was held at Shea Stadium in New York that was attended by President Bill Clinton and many other dignitaries. On that day Major League Baseball retired Jackie's No. 42, not only on the Dodgers, but on every team in baseball—perhaps the greatest honor a professional player can achieve.

Jackie Robinson paved the way for all African American major league players, but his legacy extends far beyond baseball. As early as 1949, he was a vocal champion for civil rights, testifying in front of Congress about discrimination. He served on the board of the National Association for the Advancement of Colored People (NAACP) until 1967. After his death his wife, Rachel, established the Jackie Robinson Foundation, dedicated to helping young minorities achieve success through mentoring and scholarship programs.

The sport of baseball has seen some amazing players. Most experts will tell you that Babe Ruth changed baseball. But Jackie Robinson changed America. Now *that's* a legacy.

WARREN SPAHN

So if Cy Young won more games than any right-handed pitcher in history, who is the lefty champion? A hint comes from a funny rhyme from the 1948 season. The Boston Braves were in the thick of the National League pennant race, and a sportswriter came up with the following suggestion for the Braves. To have their best chance to win the pennant, their pitching rotation should be, "Spahn and Sain and pray for rain." "Spahn" was Warren Spahn, and "Sain" was Johnny Sain. They were the two best pitchers on the team. And during a couple of weeks in September, one or the other pitched just about every day unless the game got rained out. In one of those games, Warren pitched fourteen innings as the Braves beat the Brooklyn Dodgers 2–1. That win put the Braves in first place for good as they went on to win their first pennant in 34 years.

But let's go back to the beginning. Warren Spahn was born in Buffalo, New York, in 1921. His father was a semipro baseball player, and he built a pitcher's mound in their backyard. Warren developed a high leg kick, which made it difficult for the batter to quickly see the baseball as it was being thrown toward home plate. Warren made it to the major leagues in 1942 at the age of 21. He got to pitch in a couple of games, but nothing special happened, and he didn't pitch in the big leagues again for four years because of World War II.

Warren was drafted into the Army in 1943, and he wound up fighting in some very famous battles. You may have heard of the Battle of the Bulge. It was one of the bloodiest battles of the war, in which over 19,000 Americans were killed. But Warren not only

WARREN SPAHN

BORN: April 23, 1921

BIRTHPLACE: Buffalo, NY

HEIGHT: 6'0" **WEIGHT:** 175 lbs.

TEAMS: Boston Braves, Milwaukee Braves, New York Mets, San Francisco Giants

BATS: Left **THROWS:** Left

POSITION: Pitcher

ROOKIE YEAR: 1942

CAREER ERA: 3.09

CAREER HIGHLIGHTS: Voted to 17 All-Star Games from 1947 to 1963; led the National League in strikeouts for four consecutive years from 1949 to 1952; won the Cy Young Award in 1957; led the National League in wins for five consecutive years from 1957 to 1961; pitched a no-hitter in 1960 and 1961; uniform number (No. 21) was retired in 1965; inducted into the Hall of Fame in 1973

He stood only 6 foot tall and weighed 175 pounds, but he combined that high leg kick with incredible accuracy. His pitches would nibble at the corners or dart just outside the strike zone. He once said that "home plate is 17 inches wide. I give the batter the middle 13 inches. But the two outside inches on either side belong to me. That's where I throw the ball."

And throw the ball he did. That first year after the war, he had an ordinary 8–5 record, but then—look out! The following season he really made a name for himself, winning

21 games with seven shutouts. He also had the best earned run average (ERA) in the National League, 2.33. It was the first of 13 seasons in which Warren won 20 or more games. That's a record for lefty pitchers.

survived, he became a hero. He was awarded a Bronze Star and a Purple Heart.

He returned to the Boston Braves after the war and won his first major league game in 1946. He was already 25 years old, but he was just beginning an amazing pitching career that would last another 19 seasons. Warren wasn't the biggest or the fastest pitcher around.

Warren Spahn winds up for a pitch during practice.

Now let's get back to that 1948 season, when it was "Spahn and Sain and pray for rain." In the World Series, the Braves took on the Cleveland Indians. After Johnny Sain was the winning pitcher in Game 1, Warren was the losing pitcher in Game 2. The Indians were hot, also winning Games 3 and 4. Game 5 was in Cleveland, as the Indians went for the clinching win. When the Braves fell behind 5–4 in the fourth inning, Warren was brought in to pitch from the bullpen. Cleveland never scored another run. The Braves stayed alive, winning 11–5. But the next day, it ended. The Indians won the World Series in six games.

The two best pitchers on the 1948 National League champion Boston Braves were Warren Spahn (L) and Johnny Sain.

Warren didn't get to another World Series until 1957. He would win 20 or more games just about every season, but the Braves weren't good enough to win the pennant. One game in June 1952 was typical. Warren struck out 18 Cubs and pitched all fifteen innings, but the Braves lost the game 3–1. The only Braves run came on a home run by Warren. That year the Braves finished 32 games out of first place. After the season, the team moved to Milwaukee.

Milwaukee is where Warren achieved some of his biggest triumphs. That very day in 1952 when Warren was losing that fifteen-inning game to the Cubs, the Braves signed a young star named Hank Aaron. Led by Warren's pitching and Aaron's hitting, the Braves became a National League powerhouse.

That first year in Milwaukee, Warren led the league with 23 wins and a 2.10 ERA. The Braves went from next-to-last place to second. And Warren didn't let up. In 1957 he won 21 games as Milwaukee won the pennant and Warren won the Cy Young Award for being the best pitcher in baseball. In the World Series, the Braves faced the defending champs, the Yankees. In Game 1, Warren was outpitched by another great lefty, Whitey Ford. But Warren was the winning pitcher in Game 4 as the Braves won the World Series in seven games.

The following year the same two teams met in the 1958 World Series. This time Warren got his revenge on Ford. The two lefties locked up in Games 1 and 4, and Warren was the winning pitcher in both games. However, the Yankees wound up winning that World Series in seven games.

It was Warren's last World Series, but he was far from through. In 1960 he pitched a no-hitter against the Phillies, and the following year, at the age of 40, he pitched another one against the Giants. In 1963, at the age of 42, he tied his career best by winning 23 games. During that season he was involved in one of the most remarkable games of all time.

It was July 2 in San Francisco, and Warren was pitching against Juan Marichal of the Giants. It was 0–0 after nine innings. The Giants manager, Alvin Dark, kept visiting the mound to talk with Marichal as the game went on and on. But Marichal refused to leave the game.

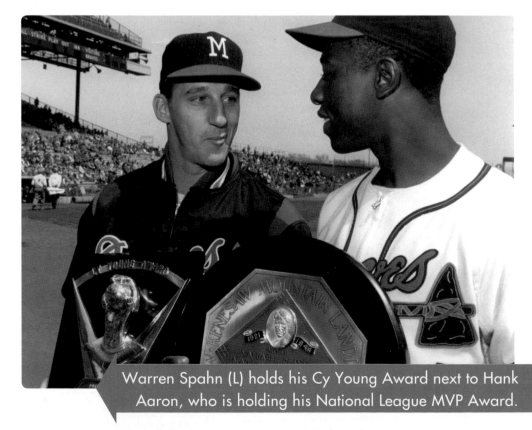

Warren Spahn (L) holds his Cy Young Award next to Hank Aaron, who is holding his National League MVP Award.

He argued that Warren was 42, and he was only 25. He didn't want to be shown up by an "old man." The game dragged on for four hours before Willie Mays of the Giants finally won it with a home run in the bottom of the sixteenth inning to make the final score 1–0. Nowadays pitchers are often taken out of a game around the sixth or seventh inning after throwing 100 pitches. That day in 1963, both pitchers stayed in the game the entire sixteen innings. Marichal threw 227 pitches, and Warren threw 201. Unbelievable!

When he finally hung 'em up, Warren had set the lefty record for wins, with 363, and he had appeared in 14 All-Star Games. No pitcher has appeared in the All-Star Game more often. And the honors poured in. His No. 21 was retired by the Braves. They also unveiled a bronze statue of Warren that shows his high leg kick. The statue stands outside Turner Field in Atlanta, where the Braves now play. In addition, a street in Buffalo near Warren's high school is named after him.

Stan Musial once said, "I don't think Spahn will ever get into the Hall of Fame. He'll never stop pitching."

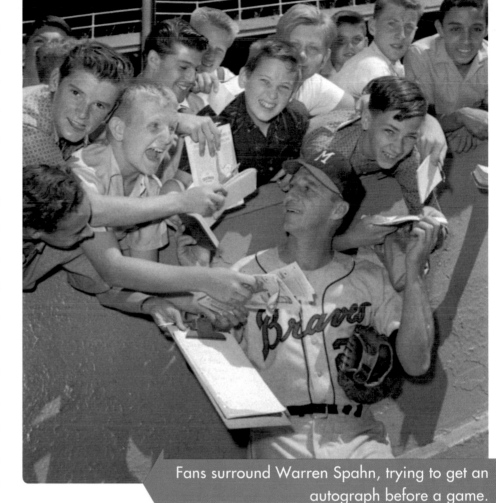

Fans surround Warren Spahn, trying to get an autograph before a game.

300 WINS CLUB

Total Wins

363

Warren Spahn also shows up in the record books for hitting. He holds the record for **MOST CAREER HOME RUNS HIT BY A PITCHER**, with 35!

Well, in 1965 after 21 seasons, Warren finally did stop at the age of 44. He was a first-ballot Hall of Famer.

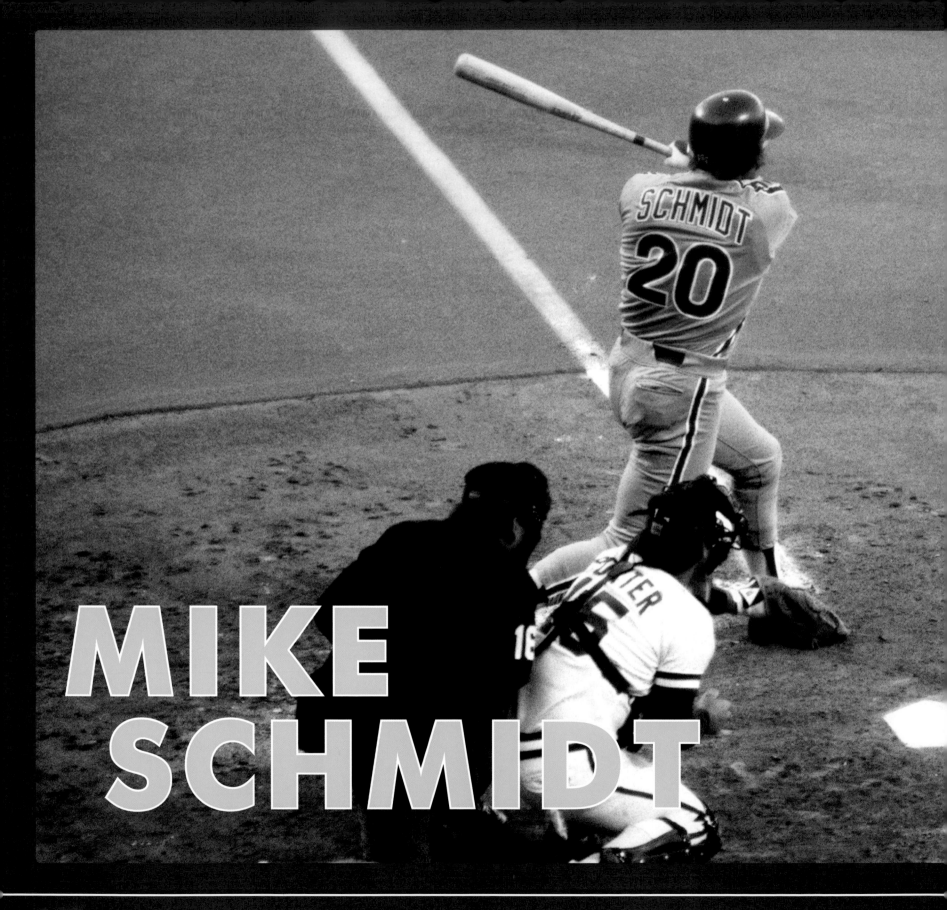

MIKE SCHMIDT

Third base is called "the hot corner," because if a righty batter hits a hard smash, the third baseman doesn't have much time to react. You have to have great reflexes to play the position, and it just may be that Mike Schmidt was the best to ever play the hot corner. He won the Gold Glove for fielding 10 times in his 18-year career. He had a strong arm and was particularly good at coming in on a slow roller, fielding the ball barehanded, and throwing out the runner at first. But that's not the only reason why he's one of the 25 greatest baseball players of all time. His 548 career home runs have a lot to do with it, too—although he should have had at least 549. But more on that in a moment.

Mike grew up in Dayton, Ohio, and played baseball for Ohio University. The Philadelphia Phillies drafted him in the second round in 1971, and he never left the Phillies organization. After a rather average season in 1973, he really broke out in 1974. That was the first time he led the National League in homers, with 36. He went on to lead the league in home runs seven more times. It was during that 1973 season that he should have hit at least one more homer.

The Phillies were playing a game at the Houston Astrodome in June. In the top of the first inning, with two men on, Mike crushed a pitch to deep center field. It was so high that it hit a speaker hanging from the Astrodome roof. The speaker was 329 feet away from home plate and 117 feet in the air. Nobody had ever hit it before.

It was estimated that if the ball hadn't hit the speaker, it would have traveled over 500 feet! When Mike hit the ball, everyone figured it was a home run, so he went into his home-run trot. But the Astrodome rules stated that the speaker was part of the field of play. So when the ball fell to the ground, it was "alive." As a result Mike probably hit the longest single in the history of baseball.

After leading the National League in homers in 1974 and 1975, 1976 started off amazing. In the Phillies' first 15 games, Mike hit 12 homers. During that streak he did something that's been done less than 10 times in major league history.

It was April 17 at Wrigley Field in Chicago, and the Phillies beat the Cubs 18–16.

Mike Schmidt hits his second home run of the game against the Chicago Cubs, leading the Phillies to a 23–22 victory.

MIKE SCHMIDT'S BATTING STANCE WAS UNIQUE. He virtually turned his back to the pitcher. He did strike out a lot, but when he uncoiled, there was always the chance that he'd hit a homer.

In the top of the fifth, with the Phillies trailing 13–2, Mike hit a two-run homer. In the seventh he hit another homer to close the gap to 13–7. And the next inning he hit his third homer of the game, a three-run shot, making the score 13–12. Mike came up again in the tenth inning with the score tied 15–15, and he belted his fourth straight homer! It was an incredibly rare feat indeed.

The Phillies were now on a roll. They made the playoffs in 1976, 1977, and 1978. That initial trip to the playoffs in 1976 was their first time in postseason play since 1950. Along the way Mike starting hitting to all fields. Earlier in his career, he was a dead pull hitter, hitting everything to left field. Now he was becoming more dangerous. It all came together in one magical season for the Phillies: 1980.

In 1980 Mike hit 48 home runs. That set a record for

third basemen. (It has since been broken in the American League by Alex Rodriguez.) But Mike also led the National League in runs batted in (RBIs), and he achieved his best batting average yet, .286, earning him his first Most Valuable Player (MVP) Award. That year the Phillies were in a dogfight for the National League East title with Montreal. Philadelphia finally clinched the division on the next-to-last day of the season in Montreal, when Mike hit a two-run homer in the eleventh inning.

The Phillies then beat the Houston Astros in five games to win the National League pennant. Philadelphia had earned a trip to the World Series for the first time in 30 years.

The Phillies played the Kansas City Royals for the championship. What a World Series it was for Mike! He batted .381, hit two homers, and drove in seven runs. The Phillies won the World Series in six games, and Mike was named the World Series MVP. The city of Philadelphia went wild! It was their first-ever baseball world championship, and the city staged an incredible parade. Fans climbed light poles, trees—anything they could find to get a glimpse of their heroes.

MIKE SCHMIDT hit 35 or more homers in 11 seasons. Only **BABE RUTH** did it more—12 seasons.

500 HOME RUNS CLUB
Total Home Runs
548

Mike Schmidt jumps onto his teammates' shoulders after the Phillies win the 1980 World Series against the Kansas City Royals.

Mike Schmidt reaches into the stands to catch a foul ball and ends up making the catch for the out!

A powerful hit from Mike Schmidt cracks his bat on a pitch during the 1983 World Series.

And the number one hero of all was Mike Schmidt.

Mike won the National League MVP Award again the following season. And in 1983 he hit 40 homers as the Phillies made it back to the playoffs. They faced the Dodgers in the National League Championship Series. In the first game, Mike hit a homer in the top of the first inning. It was the only run of the game. Mike was on a tear, batting .467 as the Phillies beat the Dodgers in four games. But in the World Series, Mike cooled off, and the Phillies got beaten by Baltimore in five. That 1983 season marked the 100th year for the Phillies. The fans were asked to vote for the greatest player in the history of the franchise. Need you ask? Mike Schmidt was the hands-down winner.

Mike never made it back to the World Series after that, but his career lasted six more years. In 1986 he won his third MVP award. And the next year, he reached a cherished milestone. On April 18, 1987, the Phillies were visiting

A few of the Major League Baseball players who can proudly claim to be part of the 500 Club.

MIKE SCHMIDT

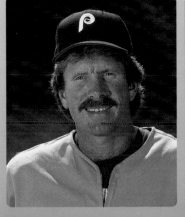

BORN: September 27, 1949

BIRTHPLACE: Dayton, OH

HEIGHT: 6'2" **WEIGHT:** 203 lbs.

TEAM: Philadelphia Phillies

BATS: Right

THROWS: Right

POSITION: Third base

ROOKIE YEAR: 1972

CAREER BATTING AVERAGE: .267

THE 25 GREATEST BASEBALL PLAYERS OF ALL TIME

CAREER HIGHLIGHTS: Voted to 12 All-Star Games from 1974 to 1989; won the Rawlings Gold Glove every year from 1976 to 1984 and in 1986; voted the National League MVP in 1980, 1981, and 1986; voted the World Series MVP in 1980; uniform number (No. 20) was retired in 1990; inducted into the Hall of Fame in 1995

Pittsburgh. In the top of the ninth, the score was tied 6–6 when Mike came to the plate. There were two men on base, and Mike was one home run shy of an exclusive club. The Pirates' Don Robinson was on the mound, and Mike worked the count to 3–0.

The great Phillies announcer Harry Kalas was at the microphone, and he screamed: "the 3–0 pitch… a long drive…there it is…number 500 for Michael Jack Schmidt!" Mike had not only won the game with a three-run homer, but he had joined a unique group of sluggers, many of whom are in this book. He was now part of the 500 Home Run Club.

Mike retired in 1989 at the age of 39. At the news conference to announce his retirement, he broke down in tears. He finished with some amazing numbers. In addition to his 548 homers, three MVP Awards, and 10 Gold Gloves, he was selected to play in the All-Star Game 12 times. He was elected to the baseball Hall of Fame in 1995, the first year he was eligible.

When the Phillies retired his No. 20 in 1990, Mike told the sold-out stadium, "My dream started on a playground near my home and came true here on this field."

It *was* a dream career come true, for sure!

HANK
AARON

At the end of every baseball season, the Hank Aaron Award is presented to the best hitter in baseball. It's quite an honor. But the phrase "best hitter" doesn't even begin to scratch the surface when you're talking about Hank. He was so much more than that.

Hank grew up in the 1930s in Mobile, Alabama. He was so poor that he couldn't afford baseball equipment, so he would practice baseball by taking bottle caps and hitting them with broom handles. Also, nobody taught him how to bat properly, so he hit cross-handed—as a righty hitter, he would mistakenly put his left hand on top of his right. He was so talented that he won a batting championship hitting cross-handed!

That remarkable accomplishment happened in the Negro Leagues, where Hank began his baseball career. At the time, the major leagues were only just beginning to allow black players. Blacks were discriminated against, and this played a big part in Hank's baseball life.

It didn't take long for Hank to be discovered by the big leagues. He signed on with the Braves in 1952. They quickly corrected his cross-handed batting style, and he showed up in spring training in 1954, hoping to make it to the big leagues. That's when he got a huge break. Another outfielder broke his leg, and the very next day, Hank started a spring-training game for the first time. Wouldn't you know it? He cracked a long home run. As it is often said in sports, "the rest is history." Let me tell you about some of that amazing history.

His rookie season was okay. He batted a respectable .280 and hit 13 homers. After that, things started to heat up. In 1955, at the age of 21, he batted .314 and led the league in doubles. It was just his second major league season—yet he was voted to the All-Star team that year.

HANK "HAMMERIN' HANK" AARON

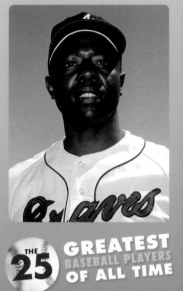

BORN: February 5, 1934

BIRTHPLACE: Mobile, AL

HEIGHT: 6'0" **WEIGHT:** 180 lbs.

TEAMS: Milwaukee Braves, Atlanta Braves, Milwaukee Brewers

BATS: Right **THROWS:** Right

POSITION: Outfielder

ROOKIE YEAR: 1954

CAREER BATTING AVERAGE: .305

CAREER HIGHLIGHTS: Voted to every All-Star Game from 1955 to 1975; won the Gold Glove in 1958, 1959, and 1960; voted the National League MVP in 1957; holds the second-highest all-time career home-run record (755); first player to beat Babe Ruth's career home-run record; uniform number (No. 44) was retired in 1976; inducted into the Hall of Fame in 1982

Hank Aaron waits for a pitch during a game against the St. Louis Cardinals.

The next year was even better. In 1956 he got 200 hits and won his first batting title, hitting .328. But 1957 was a magical year in Hank's career. He was all of 23 years old, and he was unstoppable. He belted 44 homers (which is also the number he wore) and drove in 132 runs. He led the National League in both categories and came close to winning the Triple Crown. He finished third in batting with a .322 average. As a result he won his one and only National League Most Valuable Player (MVP) Award.

More importantly, the Braves were in a pennant race, and on September 23, Milwaukee hosted St. Louis. With the score 2–2 in the eleventh inning, Hank hit a pennant-clinching, two-run homer. It was the first pennant won by the Milwaukee Braves. His teammates mobbed him at home plate and carried him off the field.

In the 1957 World Series, the Braves faced the defending world champs, the New York Yankees—and

Hank was the star. He hit three homers with seven runs batted in (RBIs) and batted .393. The Braves gave the city of Milwaukee its first world championship, beating the Yankees in seven games.

Hank followed up that amazing 1957 season with a terrific 1958 season. He led the Braves to another pennant, but this time in the World Series, the Yankees emerged victorious in seven games. Little did anyone realize that 1958 would be the last time Hank would play in a World Series.

Even though Hank never made it to the fall classic again, he still compiled some incredible records. In 1963 he came even closer to winning the Triple Crown. He missed winning the batting title by just seven points. But most of all, he was consistent. He credited Jackie Robinson for that. Early in Hank's career, Robinson had said to him that "baseball was a game you played every day, not once a week." Year in and year out, he would lead the league in one category of hitting or another, and the numbers were astounding. Before he was done, Hank would set the major league records for RBIs, extra-base hits, and total bases. These are records that still stand today. Without throwing too many stats at you, during his career he played in 3,298 games and drove in 2,297 runs! That's unbelievable. But what was really unbelievable was his assault on baseball's most hallowed record.

Babe Ruth held the career home-run record from the day he retired in 1935, with 714. It was a record that many predicted would never be broken. And the truth is Hank wasn't really thought of as a

3,000 HITS CLUB

Total Hits

3,771

Hank Aaron races to first base after a successful bunt.

Hank Aaron's teammates congratulate him after he ties the all-time home run record of 714.

Hank Aaron accepts a trophy after hitting his 714th career home run.

home-run hitter. Sure, he hit a lot of them, but the most he ever hit in a season was 44, and he only led the National League in homers four times. But over time the numbers kept piling up. When the 1970s rolled around, fans starting taking notice. He had passed the 500 home-run plateau in 1968. (He was the first player to hit 500 homers and amass 3,000 hits.) Three years later he became just the third player to reach 600. And then the chase was on to catch Ruth. That was when things turned nasty.

There were narrow-minded people in the United States who didn't want to see a black man beat the record of a white baseball hero. So Hank received lots and lots of hate mail. When the 1973 season ended, Hank had hit 713 homers. He needed just one more to equal Ruth. During that winter things really got ugly as Hank received death threats. Babe Ruth's wife helped to quiet things down. She said her husband would have been rooting for Hank to break his record.

It happened on the night of April 8, 1974. The Braves were hosting the Dodgers. In the fourth inning, Hank hit a long drive

500 HOME RUNS CLUB
Total Home Runs
755

to left field that cleared the fence. The crowd went wild. Fireworks were shot into the sky. The "unbreakable" mark of 714 had been shattered. Hank was the new home-run champion. The game was stopped, and a ceremony was held at home plate in honor of Hank breaking Ruth's cherished record. He went on to finish his career with 755 homers. (Barry Bonds now holds the record, with 762.)

Here's the part I liked best about Hank. He was a quiet man who never called attention to himself. He just went about doing his job and tried to make things better. He's been a lifelong crusader for integration. I consider it an honor to have met Hank. Hank once wrote a book called *I Had a Hammer*. (His nickname was "Hammerin' Hank.") I have an autographed copy, and I consider it to be one of my most prized possessions.

Has there ever been a player who has been honored more?

When Hank was elected to the Baseball Hall of Fame, he received 97.8 percent of the votes—second only to Ty Cobb. He received medals from two different presidents, and there are no less than three statues of Hank standing outside various baseball stadiums. Of course, the Braves retired his No. 44, and he even had his picture on a box of Wheaties!

And in that town of Mobile, Alabama, where he hit

Outside the Brewers ball park is a statue of Hall of Famer Hank Aaron.

bottle caps with broomsticks as a kid, the name of the ballpark is Hank Aaron Stadium.

Hank was the classic five-tool player. He could hit, hit with power, field (he won three Gold Gloves in right field), throw, and run. And it's just possible that he was even a better person than he was a player.

ALEX RODRIGUEZ

Two players in this book have not been elected to the Baseball Hall of Fame. Pete Rose is ineligible, because he is banned from baseball for betting on games. The other player is Alex Rodriguez. That's because at the time this book was written, Alex was still playing.

My Blue Ribbon Panel decided that Alex was one of the 25 greatest players of all time, even though they didn't know what his final statistics would be. That's how terrific a player he is. For a good portion of his career, he was widely considered to be "the best player in baseball."

Alex was born in New York City in 1975. His family first moved to the Dominican Republic and then to Miami. That's where his love of sports took off. At the Boys and Girls Club, Alex won two national baseball titles. Then in high school, he was not only good at baseball, he played on the basketball team and was the starting quarterback on the football team. But he turned his full attention to baseball when he batted .505 his senior year in high school and was named an All-American.

Next up was the pros. Alex was the top draft pick of the Seattle Mariners and made it to the big leagues when he was just 18 years old! By the age of 20, he was the starting shortstop for the Mariners. And in his first full major league season, Alex hit 36 home runs, drove in 123 runs, and won the American League batting title when he hit an astounding .358. That year he was the youngest shortstop to ever play in an All-Star Game.

That was just the beginning. There wasn't a season that went by that Alex didn't do something amazing. In 1997 in a game in Detroit, the Mariners beat the Tigers 14–6. Alex hit a homer in his first time at bat. In the fourth inning, he singled. He hit a triple

Alex Rodriguez was one of the best shortstops in baseball during the first 10 years of his career, but when he moved to the Yankees, he had to switch to playing third base. That's because the Yankees already had an All-Star shortstop in Derek Jeter.

Derek Jeter (No. 2) congratulates Alex Rodriguez after Alex hits a two-run homer against the Boston Red Sox.

After the 2000 season, Alex became a free agent, and he signed with the Texas Rangers. It was a 10-year contract worth a record $252 million dollars. He continued to do incredible things. His first season in Texas, he hit 52 homers. That was a record for shortstops. And in 2002 he broke his own record when he hit 57! The next season he won his first American League Most Valuable Player (MVP) Award. Along the way he picked up the catchy nickname "A-Rod." But while he was piling up all those great numbers, his team wasn't winning. Alex had now been in the majors for 10 seasons, and while he had been to the playoffs three times with Seattle, he had never been to the World Series.

He figured that would change in 2004, when he was traded to the Yankees in a blockbuster deal. The Yankees had been to the World Series six of the previous eight years, winning it four times. And now "the best player in baseball" was joining the team.

It certainly looked like the Yankees were heading back to the World Series that year. They led Boston three games to none in the American League Championship Series. Then in an astonishing turn of events, the Red Sox swept the next four games. The Yankees were shocked. For the next three seasons, they were eliminated in the first round of the

in the eighth, so when he came up to bat in the ninth, he needed a double to become the first Mariner to hit for the cycle (single, double, triple, and home run in a nine-inning game). And wouldn't you know? He did it!

Alex Rodriguez poses with Babe Ruth's daughter Julia after receiving the Babe Ruth Home Run Award.

ALEX "A-ROD" RODRIGUEZ

BORN: July 27, 1975

BIRTHPLACE: New York, NY

HEIGHT: 6'3" **WEIGHT:** 190 lbs.

TEAMS: Seattle Mariners, Texas Rangers, New York Yankees

BATS: Right **THROWS:** Right

POSITION: Shortstop, Third Base

ROOKIE YEAR: 1994

CAREER BATTING AVERAGE (THROUGH 2009): .305

THE 25 GREATEST BASEBALL PLAYERS OF ALL TIME

CAREER HIGHLIGHTS: Voted to every All-Star Game from 1996 to 1998 and from 2000 to 2008; won the Hank Aaron Award for the American League in 2001, 2002, 2003, and 2007; won the Major League Player of the Year in 1996, 2002, and 2007; voted the American League MVP in 2003, 2005, and 2007

playoffs, and Alex took a lot of criticism. He would pile up amazing numbers in the regular season, but when the calendar turned to October, he struggled.

In 2005, for example, he hit 48 homers, which was the most for any right-handed batter in Yankee history. He won his second MVP Award that season. In 2007 he started red-hot. He hit six home runs in the first seven games. He hit two game-winning homers before the season was even 15 games old. That season he also became the youngest player (32 years old) to hit his 500th career homer, and he won his third MVP Award. But once again he came up empty in the postseason.

Where he didn't struggle was in his bank account. After the 2007 season, A-Rod signed an even bigger contract than the one before. It was another record-breaker: 10 years, $275 million. Despite all his records, the Yankees failed to make the playoffs in 2008.

The 2009 season couldn't have started worse. Alex admitted that he had used performance-enhancing drugs when he played for Texas. The drugs, known as steroids, are now illegal in baseball, but there were no rules against them during the time he admitted using them. Nonetheless many fans were unhappy. They felt that players who used steroids were cheating. And the year got worse for Alex. He had a hip injury and missed the start of the season. But he returned with a bang.

On the first pitch he saw upon returning in May, he hit a three-run homer. And he didn't let up. In the last game of the season against Tampa Bay, Alex needed two homers and seven runs batted in (RBIs) to reach 30 home runs and 100 RBIs for the season. He did it all in one inning! In the top of the sixth, he hit a three-run homer, and before the inning was over, he hit a grand slam. The

Alex Rodriguez is safe at second after batting a double.

seven RBIs in one inning set an American League record. It enabled him to reach 30 homers and 100 RBIs for a record 13 times. Babe Ruth had done it 12 times. And the Yankees made it back to the playoffs.

To show you how much Alex had struggled in the postseason, since 2004 he had come to bat 29 times with runners on base—and he didn't have a single hit. That was about to change in a hurry.

In the first round of the playoffs against Minnesota, he had two RBIs in the first game and three more in the second, including a game-tying two-run homer in the ninth inning. He also hit a homer in Game 3 as the Yankees swept the Twins in three games. Next up in the American League Championship Series were the Los Angeles Angels of Anaheim.

Alex Rodriguez had always worn No. 3, but when he was traded to New York, he couldn't wear that number! You see, No. 3 was Babe Ruth's number, and it had been retired by the Yankees. So Alex took No. 13.

In the second game, the Yanks were trailing 2–1 in the bottom of the eleventh inning when A-Rod struck again. He hit another huge homer. The Yanks went on to win the game and the pennant in six games. For the series Alex had three homers and batted .429. His postseason problems had evaporated in a big way, and for the first time, he was going to the World Series.

It was the Yankees against the defending champion Phillies. In Game 3, Alex hit his first World Series homer. Then in Game 4, Alex had the tie-breaking hit in the ninth inning as the Yankees won 7–4 and took a commanding lead, three games to one.

Two days later A-Rod and the Yankees won the World Series in six games. What a relief for Alex! A season that had begun with an admission of cheating and an injury had ended with a trip up the Canyon of Heroes, the historic location of New York City's ticker-tape parades, as the city celebrated the Yankees' 27th world championship.

By the end of the 2009 season, Alex's name was already written all over the record book. He had won three MVP Awards and two Gold Gloves, he was named to 12 All-Star teams, and he was also the salary king—all fitting for a player often called "the best player in baseball." But finally he could be called something that meant more than all of the other stuff combined: world champion!

After driving in the go-ahead run in the ninth inning of Game 4 of the 2009 World Series , Alex Rodriguez celebrates with Derek Jeter.

JOE
DIMAGGIO

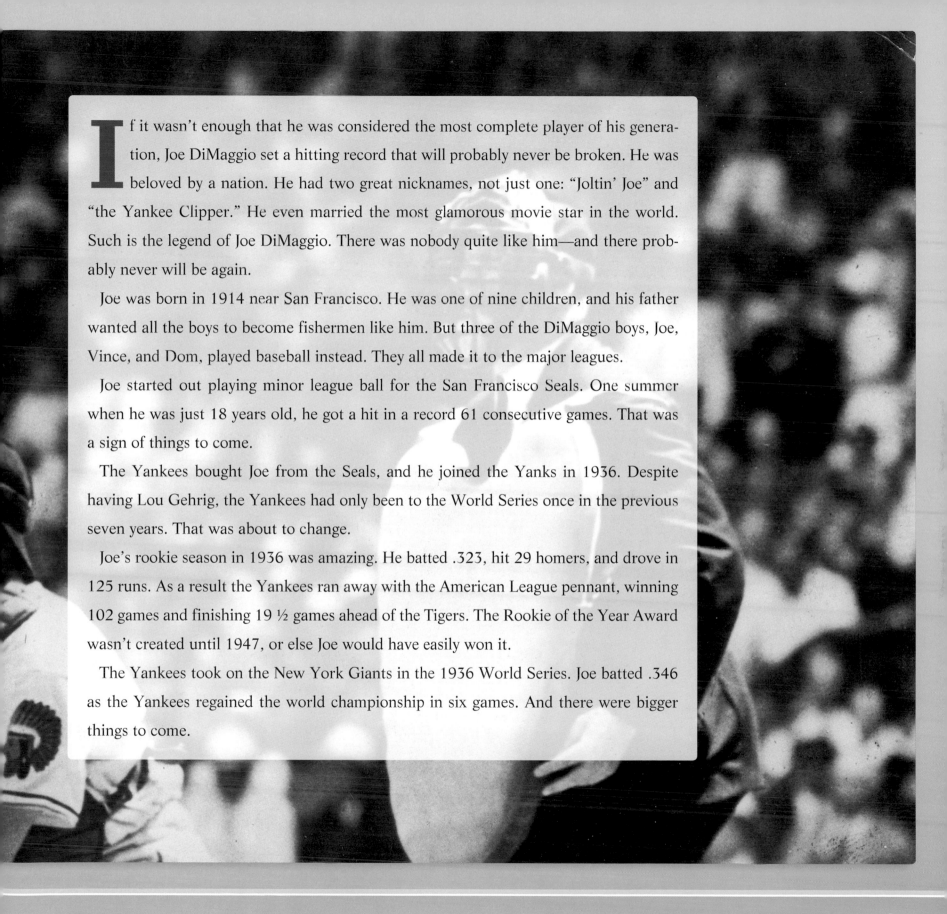

If it wasn't enough that he was considered the most complete player of his generation, Joe DiMaggio set a hitting record that will probably never be broken. He was beloved by a nation. He had two great nicknames, not just one: "Joltin' Joe" and "the Yankee Clipper." He even married the most glamorous movie star in the world. Such is the legend of Joe DiMaggio. There was nobody quite like him—and there probably never will be again.

Joe was born in 1914 near San Francisco. He was one of nine children, and his father wanted all the boys to become fishermen like him. But three of the DiMaggio boys, Joe, Vince, and Dom, played baseball instead. They all made it to the major leagues.

Joe started out playing minor league ball for the San Francisco Seals. One summer when he was just 18 years old, he got a hit in a record 61 consecutive games. That was a sign of things to come.

The Yankees bought Joe from the Seals, and he joined the Yanks in 1936. Despite having Lou Gehrig, the Yankees had only been to the World Series once in the previous seven years. That was about to change.

Joe's rookie season in 1936 was amazing. He batted .323, hit 29 homers, and drove in 125 runs. As a result the Yankees ran away with the American League pennant, winning 102 games and finishing 19 ½ games ahead of the Tigers. The Rookie of the Year Award wasn't created until 1947, or else Joe would have easily won it.

The Yankees took on the New York Giants in the 1936 World Series. Joe batted .346 as the Yankees regained the world championship in six games. And there were bigger things to come.

Joe DiMaggio begins the race to first base after hitting the ball.

The summer of 1941 was unforgettable for Joe. On May 15, he got a base hit. No big deal. But day after day, he kept getting hits. The record for hits in consecutive games was 44, and it was set way back in 1897. Joe smashed that record and kept on going. He reached 56 consecutive games! During that streak he batted .408. No player had ever been hotter.

Finally on July 17 in Cleveland, the record streak came to an end. It took two great plays by Indians third baseman Ken Keltner to keep Joe out of the hit column. Then the next game, Joe started a 16-game hitting streak. He finished the season batting .357, and he was honored with his second MVP

The next year Joe led the major leagues in homers, with 46, and he continued to be a hitting machine. He was so good that he rarely struck out. In 1939 he led the majors in hitting with an astounding .381 average. That year he won his first Most Valuable Player (MVP) Award. And as Joe went, so went the Yankees. In his first four seasons, the Yankees won four pennants and four World Series. Not a bad way to start a career.

In 1941 Joe DiMaggio had a hit in each of
56 CONSECUTIVE GAMES.

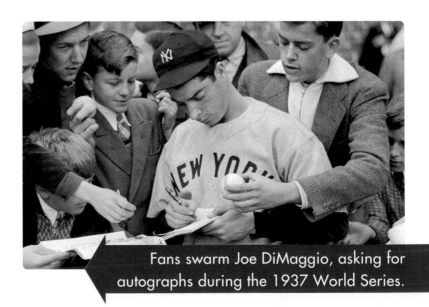

Fans swarm Joe DiMaggio, asking for autographs during the 1937 World Series.

Award. And yes, the Yankees won the World Series again—Joe's fifth championship in six years.

Joe was unbelievably consistent. During that 1941 season, he only struck out 13 times the entire year. That's incredible. In 1947 he played an entire season in center field and made just one error. He played the field so effortlessly and got such a great jump on batted balls that he almost never had to dive to make a catch. Joe himself explained why he performed at such a high level just about every game. He said, "I always thought there was at least one person in the stands who had never seen me play, and I didn't want to let him down."

Joe carried himself with dignity and grace. You never saw him get into an argument on the field, and he never displayed a temper. In Game 6 of the 1947 World Series against the Brooklyn Dodgers, Joe hit a long drive to left field in Yankee Stadium. It looked like it would be a game-tying three-run homer. But Al Gionfriddo went way back in left and made what many felt was one of the greatest catches in World Series history. Joe was nearing second base when Gionfriddo made the catch. Joe just kicked at the dirt a bit. That was it—nothing more. That was the biggest display

On June 24, 1936, Joe DiMaggio hit **TWO HOME RUNS IN THE SAME INNING!**

Joe DiMaggio competes in a pregame home-run derby.

of emotion that Joe ever showed on a baseball field.

Between 1936 and 1951, Joe led the Yankees to the World Series 10 times, and they won nine of them. The number might have been even more, but Joe missed three years because of World War II. Along the way Joe won 3 MVP Awards and was named to the All-Star team in each and every one of the 13 seasons he played. No other player can make that claim. He was so revered as a player that he won the MVP Award in 1947 despite the fact that Ted Williams won the Triple Crown that year for the Boston Red Sox.

In 1949 Joe broke another record. He became the first player to make $100,000. Can you imagine what he'd be worth today? Joe used to joke about what his contract negotiations would be like if he were playing in the big-money free-agent era. He said that if he were playing, he'd walk in to negotiate with the Yankees owner, throw his arm around his shoulder, and say, "Hi, partner." In other words Joe felt as if he would own part of the team!

When Joe stopped playing in 1951, he retired with a lifetime batting average of .325. He had hit 361 homers but only struck out 369 times. Compare that with Babe Ruth, for example, who hit 714 home runs but struck out nearly twice as much—1,330 times.

Needless to say, Joe was elected to the Hall of Fame. He was also presented the Presidential Medal

JOE DIMAGGIO

BORN: November 25, 1914

BIRTHPLACE: Martinez, CA

HEIGHT: 6'2" **WEIGHT:** 193 lbs.

TEAM: New York Yankees

BATS: Right

THROWS: Right

POSITION: Outfielder

ROOKIE YEAR: 1936

CAREER BATTING AVERAGE:
.325

CAREER HIGHLIGHTS: Voted to every All-Star Game from 1936 to 1942 and from 1946 to 1951; led the American League in batting in 1939 and 1940; voted the American League MVP in 1939, 1941, and 1947; uniform number (No. 5) was retired in 1952; inducted into the Hall of Fame in 1955

Marilyn Monroe poses with her new husband, Joe DiMaggio.

of Freedom by President Gerald Ford. The Yankees retired his No. 5, and they built a monument to him that sits in Monument Park in Yankee Stadium. There's even a major roadway in New York City called the Joe DiMaggio Highway.

Joe was revered as a player, but would you believe that when he retired, he became even more famous? In 1954 he married a glamorous actress, Marilyn Monroe. What a couple they made: a handsome baseball idol and a gorgeous movie star. The marriage lasted less than a year, but it just added to Joe's legend. Joe continued to stay in the public eye. He made TV commercials, and he became part of American folklore. He is mentioned in novels, songs, and even comic books.

Joe DiMaggio shakes hands with NYC mayor Fiorello LaGuardia after receiving the American League Most Valuable Player award.

Perhaps the most famous use of his name comes in a song performed by Simon & Garfunkel called "Mrs. Robinson." One of the song's lyrics: "Where have you gone, Joe DiMaggio? A nation turns its lonely eyes to you." The song came out long after Joe retired. The point of the song was that people missed a simpler time, when players like Joe DiMaggio acted like real heroes.

At the old Yankee Stadium, there used to be a sign that hung from the tunnel between the Yankee clubhouse and the dugout. It was a quote from Joe. It read, "I want to thank the Good Lord for making me a Yankee." All the players would pass under it on the way to the field.

I'll bet if you asked the millions of fans who saw him play, they would likely say, "I want to thank the Good Lord for making Joe DiMaggio a ballplayer." If he wasn't the perfect player, he was as close as one could be.

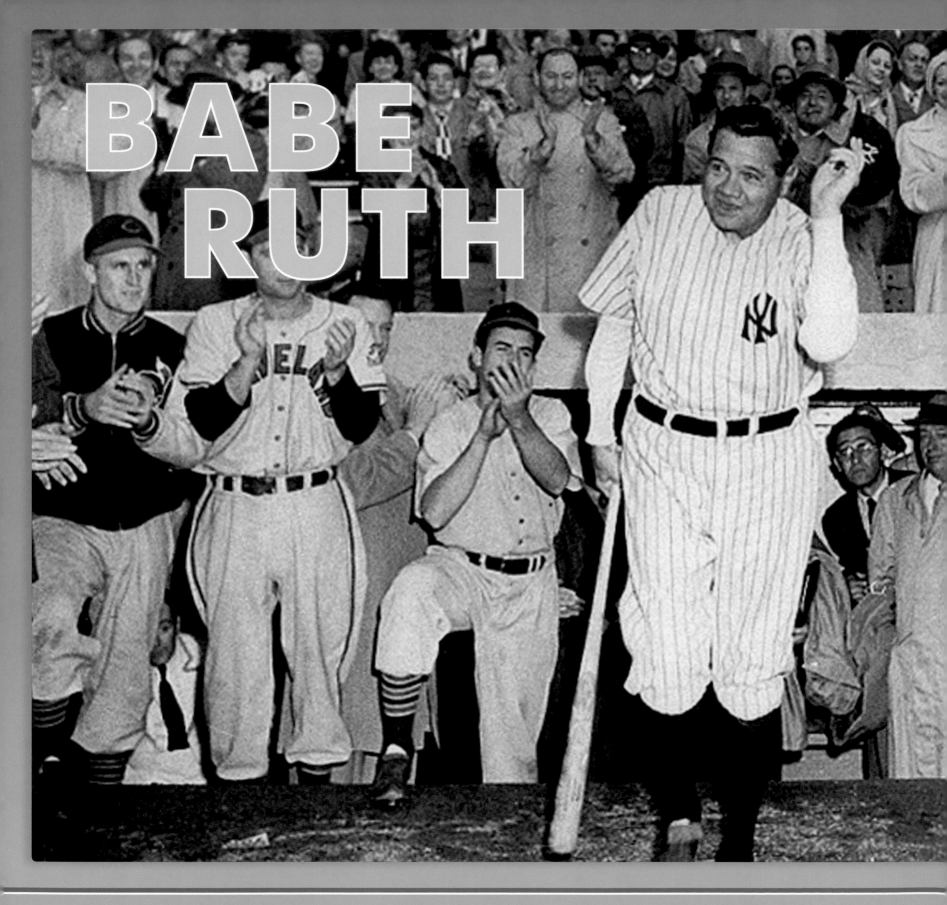

BABE
RUTH

I've saved the best for last. In writing this book, it was extremely hard to narrow down the list to just 25 players. Some of the all-time greats have been left out. It would have been even harder to rank the players 1 through 25. How can you compare players from different eras? Or pitchers with hitters? But there's no question in my mind who is the single greatest baseball player of all time: the one and only Babe Ruth.

The Babe's real name was George Herman Ruth Jr. He was born in Baltimore in 1895, and as a youngster, his parents basically abandoned him. They placed him in a reform school/orphanage called St. Mary's. That's where he started playing baseball. When he was 19, he was signed to play minor league baseball in Baltimore by a scout named Jack Dunn. He was referred to as "Jack's newest babe," and the name stuck. The Babe was mostly a pitcher and a catcher back then.

Baltimore was a minor league team for the Boston Red Sox, and after just five months in Baltimore, the Babe found himself in the big leagues. On July 11, 1914, the 19-year-old Babe made his major league debut as a pitcher, and he got the win as the Red Sox beat Cleveland 4–3. He only pitched in four games that season, but the following year, the Babe really took off with the Red Sox. Boston won the World Series in 1915, 1916, and 1918.

The Babe didn't pitch in the 1915 Series, but in his World Series debut in 1916, he set a record that still stands today. He pitched Game 2 as the Red Sox beat the Brooklyn Robins 2–1 in fourteen innings. The Babe pitched the entire game. To this day it's the longest complete-game victory in World Series history! And in the 1918 World Series, the Babe won two games. Along the way he pitched 29 ⅔ consecutive scoreless innings. That record wasn't broken until four decades later.

Yup, Babe Ruth was an incredible pitcher. He also played some games in right field. In fact, during the 1918 season he won 13 games pitching, and he led the American League

Babe Ruth takes a big swing during an exhibition game in Tokyo.

with 11 homers. The following year he was used primarily in right field, and he set a major league record with 29 homers. On the mound, he won 89 games for Boston between 1914 and 1919, including two 20-win seasons.

The Babe probably would have gone on to become one of the greatest pitchers of all time, but two things happened. First the Red Sox sold him to the Yankees for $100,000. It was easily the worst deal in the history of baseball. The Red Sox, who had won three World Series in four years, didn't win another for 86 years. Their lack of success became known as "the Curse of the Bambino." They were somehow a cursed baseball team because they let the great Babe Ruth get away. Meanwhile the Yankees became a powerhouse. The other thing that happened was in 1920—the Yankees turned this great pitcher into their everyday right fielder.

I think they made the right move. In 1920 the Babe exploded and hit 54 home runs. Remember, he held the record from the year before, with just 29. From then on he never let up. He hit 59 the following year, and then 35 in 1922. In those years the Yankees were sharing the Polo Grounds with the New York Giants. But the Yankees' new popularity, fueled by the Babe's power hitting, enabled the Yankees to build a huge new stadium of their own in the Bronx. In 1923 they moved into Yankee Stadium, which forever became known as "the House that Ruth Built." The Yankees have since moved into a new stadium, the new Yankee Stadium.

The Babe's long home runs became known as "Ruthian blasts." It's an adjective that's still used today to describe long homers.

In the original Yankee Stadium, the legend of the Babe reached Ruthian proportions. In the very first game against Boston, he hit the first home run ever hit in the new ballpark. His 41 homers and 131 runs batted in (RBIs) led the league. He also batted an astounding .393, the highest average he would ever attain, but a Tigers player named Harry Heilmann hit .403 that season, depriving the Babe of winning the Triple Crown.

In the 1923 World Series, the Babe and the Yanks became champs for the first time together. He batted .368 and hit 3 homers as the Yankees beat the Giants in 6 games. During the Babe's years with the Yankees, they won seven pennants and four World Series.

The 1927 season was simply amazing. The Yankee lineup was unstoppable. They were known as "Murderer's Row," and the Babe was the number one "killer." Not only did he hit .356, but he staged one of the legendary assaults on the record books. He already held the home-run record by hitting 59 homers in a season. Was it possible he could hit 60? He went on a tear in September, hitting 17 homers that month. On the next-to-last day of the season, he hit home-run number 60! That record that would stand for 34 years.

BABE RUTH

THE 25 GREATEST BASEBALL PLAYERS OF ALL TIME

BORN: February 6, 1895
BIRTHPLACE: Baltimore, MD
HEIGHT: 6'2" **WEIGHT:** 215 lbs.
TEAMS: Boston Red Sox, New York Yankees, Boston Braves
BATS: Left **THROWS:** Left
POSITIONS: Pitcher, outfielder
ROOKIE YEAR: 1914
CAREER BATTING AVERAGE: .342

CAREER HIGHLIGHTS: Led the American League in home runs 12 times from 1918 to 1931; voted the American League MVP in 1923; voted to the All-Star Game in 1933 and 1934; in the all-time top 10 for career batting average; holds the third-highest all-time career home-run record (714); holds the second-highest all-time career RBI record (2,217); inducted into the Hall of Fame in 1936; uniform number (No. 3) was retired in 1948

For the large personality Babe Ruth became, one nickname wasn't nearly enough. He was also called **"THE GREAT BAMBINO"** and **"THE SULTAN OF SWAT."**

The 1927 Yankees set a record by winning 110 games and won the pennant by a whopping 19 games. They rolled right over the Pittsburgh Pirates, sweeping the World Series in four games as the Babe hit two homers and batted .400. Many consider the 1927 New York Yankees, led by the one and only Babe Ruth, to be the greatest baseball team of all time.

The Babe's legend continued to grow. In the 1932 World Series, he came to bat in Wrigley Field and pointed. Some claimed he was pointing to the center-field stands. Maybe he was. He belted the next pitch into the center-field bleachers. His "called shot" became legendary. The next year the very first All-Star Game was played in Chicago. The American League won, and of course, the Babe hit the first home run in All-Star Game history.

The Babe was considered a "giant of a man." He stood 6 feet, 2 inches and weighed 215 pounds. That was

500 HOME RUNS CLUB
Total Home Runs
714

considered big at the time. But it wasn't just his physical presence. He had a larger-than-life personality, which made him one of the biggest celebrities in the world. The Babe is given credit for helping baseball become the National Pastime that it is today. The game exploded in popularity during the "Roaring Twenties," and the sight of the Babe belting home run after home run was a big reason why. After the 1934 season, the Yankees believed the Babe had little left, so they traded him to the Boston Braves.

The Babe played his last game in Pittsburgh, on May 25, 1935, and in typical Ruthian fashion he hit three homers. He retired with 714 homers—a record that would hold up for nearly 40 years. He set tons of records, and some of them still stand today, including most seasons leading the league in homers (12) and highest career slugging percentage (.690).

The Babe was part of the first class inducted into the Baseball Hall of Fame in 1936. He appeared on the radio and in the movies and even had a candy bar named after him: "Baby Ruth." When he died in 1948 at the age of 53, over 100,000 people came to Yankee Stadium to pay their respects. The funeral was held at St. Patrick's Cathedral in New York City. It was a tribute fit for a king. A national treasure—and to my mind, the greatest baseball player who ever lived—had passed away. The world would never be the same!

In 1930 the Yankees paid the Babe a king's ransom for that time—$80,000. He made more than the president of the United States, Herbert Hoover. When asked about it, the Babe responded with a classic line. He said he deserved to be paid more than the president, because "I had a better year than Hoover." And you know what? He probably did.

POSTSCRIPT

S o there you have it. *The 25 Greatest Baseball Players of All Time.* Do you agree with our choices? Go to www.ThatsSports.com, and vote for your favorites. If you vote, it could make you part of my next Blue Ribbon Panel.

Who knows? Maybe this book will turn into a "doubleheader," another edition with more great players. Thanks for reading my book. I hope you continue to enjoy the great game of baseball.

ABOUT THE AUTHOR

Photo courtesy of Norman/
Marquee Photography

Len Berman is an Emmy Award–winning sportscaster who has covered just about every major sports event, including multiple Super Bowls, World Series, and Olympics during his 40-year career in broadcasting.

He is the creator of "Spanning the World," a monthly collection of sports bloopers, which was a 20-year staple on NBC's *Today* show. He is also the creator of *Sports Fantasy*, which aired on NBC and pitted regular viewers against famous sports stars.

He is the recipient of eight Emmy Awards and has been voted New York Sportscaster of the Year six times. His daily Top 5 email is featured in the *Huffington Post* and is received by thousands around the country. This is his fifth book.

A native New Yorker, Len graduated from Syracuse University. He resides on Long Island with his wife, Jill. They have three children.